Mac and Cheese Mania

Delicious, Creamy, and Easy-to-Make Recipes for the Ultimate Macaroni and Cheese Experience, with Over 100 Variations and Toppings to Satisfy Every Craving

Adam Campbell

Copyright Material ©2023

All Rights Reserved

Without the proper written consent of the publisher and copyright owner, this book cannot be used or distributed in any way, shape, or form, except for brief quotations used in a review. This book should not be considered a substitute for medical, legal, or other professional advice.

TABLE OF CONTENTS

TABLE OF CONTENTS 3
INTRODUCTION 7
BREAKFAST MAC AND CHEESE 8
1. Macaroni and Cheese Waffle 9
2. Bacon Mac and Cheese Breakfast Casserole 11
3. Mac and Cheese Breakfast Burrito 13
4. Mac and Cheese Breakfast Hash 15
5. Mac and Cheese Breakfast Pizza 17
6. Mac and Cheese Breakfast Frittata 19
7. Mac and Cheese Breakfast Sandwich 21
8. Mac and Cheese Breakfast Bowl 23

APPETIZERS 25
9. Mac and Cheese Cups 26
10. Mac and Cheese Slider 28
11. Mac and Cheese Bites 30
12. Mac and Cheese Stuffed Mushrooms 32
13. Mac and Cheese Quesadillas 34
14. Mac and Cheese Stuffed Jalapenos 36
15. Mac and Cheese Fritters 38
16. Mac and Cheese Pizza 40
17. Mac and Cheese Grilled Cheese 42
18. Mac and Cheese Dip 44
19. Mac and Cheese Stuffed Mini Peppers 46
20. Mac and Cheese Stuffed Tomatoes 48
21. Mac and Cheese Stuffed Zucchini 50
22. Mac and Cheese Croquettes 52
23. Mac and Cheese Empanadas 54

SALADS 56
24. Garden Tuna Macaroni Salad 57
25. Seafood Macaroni Salad 59
26. **Mac and Cheese Salad with Bacon** 61

27. Southwest Mac and Cheese Salad 63
28. Mac and Cheese Salad with Ham and Peas 65
29. Caprese Mac and Cheese Salad 67
30. Bacon Ranch Mac and Cheese Salad 69
31. Greek Mac and Cheese Salad 71
32. BLT Mac and Cheese Salad 73
33. Italian Mac and Cheese Salad 75
34. Mac and Cheese Salad with Broccoli and Bacon 77
35. Caesar Mac and Cheese Salad 79
36. Mac and Cheese Salad with Tuna 81

SOUPS 83

37. Creamy Mac and Cheese Soup 84
38. Broccoli Cheddar Mac and Cheese Soup 86
39. Tomato Mac and Cheese Soup 88
40. Southwest Mac and Cheese Soup 90
41. Bacon Mac and Cheese Soup 92

MAIN COURSE 94

42. Spicy Saucy Mac and "Cheese" 95
43. Southwestern Mac and "Cheese" 97
44. Homey Mac and Cheese 99
45. Creamy Mac And Cheese With Crispy Bacon 101
46. Spinach and artichoke mac-and-cheese 104
47. Lobster Mac and Cheese 107
48. Camping Mac and Cheese 110
49. **Mac and Cheese Cups** 112
50. Queso Mac and Cheese 114
51. Macaroni and Gruyere Cheese 117
52. Macaroni and Cheese with Chicken 119
53. Chili Mac Casserole 122
54. Spinach and artichoke mac-and-cheese bake 124
55. Monterrey Mini Mac and Cheese 127
56. Cauliflower Broccoli Macaroni 129

57. Spicy Chili Mac 131
58. Microwave Mac 'n' Cheese 133
59. Pizza Mac Cheese 135
60. Baked Three Cheese Macaroni 137
61. Makeover Slow Cooked Mac 'n' Cheese 139
62. Slow Cooker Bacon Mac Cheese 141
63. Bistro Mac Cheese 143
64. Makeover Creamy Mac Cheese 145
65. Gruyère and Cheddar Mac and Cheese 147
66. RumChata Macaroni and cheese 149
67. Soul Food Macaroni and Cheese 151
68. Cheezy Tomato Macaroni 154
69. Bacon Mac 'n' cheese 156
70. Phony Macaroni and Cheese 159
71. Cauliflower & Tofu Mac and Cheese 161
72. One-Pot Turkey Chili Mac 163
73. Baked Mac And Cheeze 165
74. Mac And Chard 168
75. Cheezy Tomato Macaroni 171
76. Chili Bean Mac 173
77. Italian Macaroni Bake 175
78. Macaroni and Mixed Cheese 177
79. Gruyère and Cheddar Mac and Cheese 180
80. Food Macaroni and Cheese 182
81. Slap Ya' Mama Macaroni and cheese 185
82. Spinach and artichoke mac-and-cheese bake 187
83. Cauliflower Broccoli Macaroni 190
84. Monterrey Mini Mac and Cheese 192
85. Almond Macaroni and Cheese 194
86. Queso Mac and Cheese 196
87. Macaroni and Gruyere Cheese 199
88. Macaroni and Cheese with Chicken 201

89. Meatballs and shortcut macaroni 204
90. Macaroni and Cheese Meatloaf 206
91. Macaroni in Creamy Beef Sauce 208
92. Macaroni with strawberries 210
93. Pastitsio 212

DESSERT 215
94. Macaroni souffle 216
95. Mac and Cheese Ice Cream 218
96. Mac and Cheese Bread Pudding 220
97. Mac and Cheese Cheesecake 222
98. Mac and Cheese Blondies 224
99. Mac and Cheese with Berry Compote 226
100. Mac and Cheese with Apple and Brioche 228

CONCLUSION 230

INTRODUCTION

Get ready to indulge in the ultimate comfort food experience with this collection of over 100 creative and delicious mac and cheese recipes. From classic stovetop mac and cheese to gourmet variations loaded with bacon, lobster, and truffles, this cookbook has something for every mac and cheese lover.

In these pages, you'll discover mouth-watering recipes featuring a variety of cheeses and pasta shapes, as well as gluten-free and vegan options. Whether you're looking for a quick and easy weeknight dinner or a show-stopping dish for a special occasion, you'll find it here.

With helpful tips and tricks for making the perfect mac and cheese every time, this cookbook is a must-have for anyone who loves this classic comfort food. So grab your apron and get ready to dive into the ooey, gooey world of mac and cheese!

Macaroni and cheese, comfort food, cheese, pasta, gourmet, classic, creative, recipes, bacon, lobster, truffles, variety, gluten-free, vegan, weeknight dinner, show-stopping, tips and tricks, perfect..

BREAKFAST MAC AND CHEESE

1. <u>Macaroni and Cheese Waffle</u>

YIELD: Serves 8

INGREDIENTS
- Prepared Macaroni and Cheese (recipe follows)
- 2 large eggs
- Pinch each of salt and freshly ground black pepper
- 1 cup all-purpose flour
- 1 cup seasoned bread crumbs
- ¼ cup grated hard cheese, such as Parmesan or Pecorino Romano
- Nonstick cooking spray

1 Cut the macaroni and cheese into slices about ½ inch thick.

2 Preheat the waffle iron on medium. Preheat the oven on its lowest setting.

3 In a small bowl, beat the egg with a pinch each of salt and pepper.

4 Set out 3 shallow bowls. Measure the flour into the first. In the second bowl, place the beaten eggs. Mix the bread crumbs with the cheese in the third.

5 Take a slice of the macaroni and cheese, and, handling it gently, coat both sides in the flour. Then dunk both sides in the egg. Finally, coat both sides with the bread crumbs, pressing the mixture so it sticks. Set aside the slice and repeat with the remaining slices.

6 Coat both sides of the waffle iron grid with nonstick spray. Place the macaroni and cheese slices in the waffle iron, close the lid, and cook until heated through and golden brown, 3 minutes.

7 The extraction process can be tricky. With a silicone spatula, loosen the edges of the macaroni and cheese. Use the spatula to gently pry the macaroni and cheese from the waffle iron and then support the bottom with the spatula while you lift it out with tongs.

8 Repeat Steps 5 through 7 until all of the macaroni and cheese has been waffled. Keep the finished macaroni and cheese warm in the oven.

2. Bacon Mac and Cheese Breakfast Casserole

INGREDIENTS:

1 lb elbow macaroni
1 lb bacon, chopped
1/4 cup unsalted butter
1/4 cup all-purpose flour
4 cups whole milk
2 cups shredded cheddar cheese
Salt and pepper, to taste
6 large eggs, beaten
1/4 cup chopped green onions

INSTRUCTIONS

Preheat the oven to 375°F.
Cook the elbow macaroni according to package instructions and drain.
Cook the bacon in a skillet over medium heat until crispy.
In a large pot, melt the butter over medium heat.
Add the flour and whisk until smooth.
Gradually whisk in the milk and bring to a boil, stirring constantly.
Reduce heat and simmer for 5 minutes, or until thickened.
Add the shredded cheddar cheese and stir until melted.
Season with salt and pepper to taste.
In a large bowl, combine the cooked macaroni, cheese sauce, and beaten eggs.
Stir in the chopped bacon and green onions.
Pour the mixture into a greased 9x13 inch baking dish.
Bake for 35-40 minutes, or until golden brown and set.

3. Mac and Cheese Breakfast Burrito

INGREDIENTS:

1 cup cooked macaroni
4 large eggs
1/4 cup milk
Salt and pepper, to taste
1 tbsp unsalted butter
1/4 cup shredded cheddar cheese
2 large flour tortillas

INSTRUCTIONS

In a small bowl, whisk together the eggs, milk, salt, and pepper.
Melt the butter in a skillet over medium heat.
Add the egg mixture to the skillet and cook, stirring occasionally, until the eggs are scrambled and set.
Add the cooked macaroni to the skillet and stir to combine.
Sprinkle the shredded cheddar cheese over the top of the egg and macaroni mixture.
Heat the tortillas in the microwave or on a griddle until warm.
Spoon half of the egg and macaroni mixture onto each tortilla.
Roll up the tortillas and serve.

4. Mac and Cheese Breakfast Hash

INGREDIENTS:

1 lb cooked macaroni
1 lb breakfast sausage
1/2 cup chopped onion
1/2 cup chopped green bell pepper
Salt and pepper, to taste
4 large eggs, beaten
1/4 cup shredded cheddar cheese

INSTRUCTIONS

Cook the breakfast sausage in a skillet over medium heat until browned and cooked through.

Add the chopped onion and green bell pepper to the skillet and cook until tender.

Add the cooked macaroni to the skillet and stir to combine.

Season with salt and pepper to taste.

Pour the beaten eggs over the top of the mixture in the skillet and stir to combine.

Sprinkle the shredded cheddar cheese over the top of the mixture in the skillet.

Cover the skillet and cook over medium heat for 5-7 minutes, or until the eggs are set and the cheese is melted.

5. Mac and Cheese Breakfast Pizza

INGREDIENTS:

1 lb cooked macaroni
1/2 cup pizza sauce
1/4 cup shredded mozzarella cheese
1/4 cup shredded cheddar cheese
4 large eggs
Salt and pepper, to taste

INSTRUCTIONS

Preheat the oven to 400°F.
Spread the pizza sauce over a large pizza crust.
Sprinkle the cooked macaroni over the pizza sauce.
Sprinkle the shredded mozzarella cheese and shredded cheddar cheese over the top of the macaroni.
Bake the pizza for 10-12 minutes, or until the cheese is melted and bubbly.
Remove the pizza from the oven and crack the eggs onto the top of the pizza.
Return the pizza to the oven and bake for an additional 5-7 minutes, or until the eggs are set.
Slice the pizza into wedges and serve.

6. Mac and Cheese Breakfast Frittata

INGREDIENTS:

1 lb cooked macaroni
8 large eggs, beaten
1/2 cup milk
Salt and pepper, to taste
1/4 cup shredded cheddar cheese
1/4 cup chopped green onions

INSTRUCTIONS

Preheat the oven to 375°F.
In a large bowl, whisk together the beaten eggs, milk, salt, and pepper.
Add the cooked macaroni, shredded cheddar cheese, and chopped green onions to the bowl and stir to combine.
Pour the mixture into a greased 9-inch pie dish.
Bake for 25-30 minutes, or until the frittata is set and golden brown.
Allow the frittata to cool for a few minutes before slicing and serving.

7. Mac and Cheese Breakfast Sandwich

INGREDIENTS:

1 lb cooked macaroni
8 large eggs
Salt and pepper, to taste
1/4 cup unsalted butter
4 English muffins, split and toasted
4 slices cooked ham
4 slices American cheese

INSTRUCTIONS

In a large bowl, whisk together the eggs, salt, and pepper.
Melt the butter in a large skillet over medium heat.
Add the cooked macaroni to the skillet and stir to combine.
Pour the beaten eggs over the top of the macaroni in the skillet.
Cook the eggs and macaroni, stirring occasionally, until the eggs are scrambled and set.
To assemble the sandwiches, place a slice of ham and a slice of American cheese on the bottom half of each English muffin.
Spoon the egg and macaroni mixture onto the cheese and ham.
Top with the remaining half of the English muffin and serve.

8. Mac and Cheese Breakfast Bowl

INGREDIENTS:

1 lb cooked macaroni
4 large eggs
Salt and pepper, to taste
1/4 cup unsalted butter
1/4 cup all-purpose flour
2 cups whole milk
2 cups shredded cheddar cheese
1/2 cup diced tomatoes
1/4 cup chopped green onions

INSTRUCTIONS

In a small bowl, whisk together the eggs, salt, and pepper.
Melt the butter in a large skillet over medium heat.
Add the cooked macaroni to the skillet and stir to combine.
Pour the beaten eggs over the top of the macaroni in the skillet.
Cook the eggs and macaroni, stirring occasionally, until the eggs are scrambled and set.
In a separate pot, melt the butter over medium heat.
Add the flour and whisk until smooth.
Gradually whisk in the milk and bring to a boil, stirring constantly.
Reduce heat and simmer for 5 minutes, or until thickened.

APPETIZERS

9. Mac and Cheese Cups

INGREDIENTS

- 8 oz elbow macaroni
- 2 tbsp salted butter
- 1/4 tsp paprika (use smoked paprika if you have it)
- 2 tbsp flour
- 1/2 cup whole milk
- 8 oz sharp cheddar cheese grated
- chopped chives or scallions for garnish
- butter for greasing the pan

INSTRUCTIONS

a) Grease a non-stick: mini muffin pan very well with butter or non-stick: cooking spray. Preheat the oven to 400 degrees F.

b) Bring a pot of salted water to a boil over high heat, then cook the pasta for 2 minutes less than the package says.

c) Melt the butter and add the paprika. Add the flour and stir the mixture around for 2 minutes. While whisking, add the milk.

d) Remove the pot from the heat and add the cheeses and drained pasta, stirring it all together until the cheese and sauce are well distributed.

e) Portion your mac and cheese into the muffin cups, either with a spoon or a 3-tbsp cookie scoop.

f) Bake the mac and cheese cups for 15 minutes, until bubbling and gooey.

10. Mac and Cheese Slider

Serving Size: 12

INGREDIENTS:
- 1 Cup Macaroni pasta
- 1 tablespoon butter
- Pepper to taste
- 1 ½ teaspoons all-purpose flour
- ½ cup milk
- ¾ cup cheddar cheese, shredded
- 18 oz. Hawaiian sweet rolls
- 16 oz. barbecue shredded pork, cooked
- 1 tablespoon honey
- ½ teaspoon ground mustard
- 2 tablespoons butter, melted

Directions

a) Preheat your oven to 375 degrees F.
b) Cook the pasta according to the directions in the package.
c) Drain and set aside.
d) Add the butter to a pan over medium heat.
e) Stir in the pepper and flour.
f) Stir until smooth.
g) Bring to a boil, stirring.
h) Cook for 3 to 5 minutes.
i) Add the cheese and cook while stirring until melted.
j) Add the cooked pasta to the pan.
k) Arrange the roll bottoms in a baking pan.
l) Top with the cheese and pasta mixture, shredded pork, and roll tops.
m) In a small bowl, mix the honey, mustard and butter.
n) Brush tops with this mixture.
o) Bake in the oven for 10 minutes.

11. <u>Mac and Cheese Bites</u>

INGREDIENTS:

1 box mac and cheese
2 eggs
1/2 cup panko breadcrumbs
1/2 cup all-purpose flour
Salt and pepper

INSTRUCTIONS

Cook the mac and cheese according to the instructions on the box. Let it cool for 5-10 minutes. Add in the eggs and mix well. Using a cookie scoop, form the mixture into bite-sized balls. In a separate bowl, combine the panko breadcrumbs, flour, salt, and pepper. Roll each mac and cheese ball in the breadcrumb mixture until fully coated. Place on a baking sheet and bake at 400 degrees Fahrenheit for 15-20 minutes or until golden brown.

12. Mac and Cheese Stuffed Mushrooms

INGREDIENTS:

1 box mac and cheese
12 large mushrooms
1/4 cup grated Parmesan cheese
Salt and pepper

INSTRUCTIONS

Preheat the oven to 375 degrees Fahrenheit. Cook the mac and cheese according to the instructions on the box. Remove the stems from the mushrooms and scoop out the gills. Fill each mushroom with a spoonful of mac and cheese. Sprinkle with Parmesan cheese, salt, and pepper. Place on a baking sheet and bake for 15-20 minutes or until the mushrooms are tender and the cheese is melted.

13. <u>Mac and Cheese Quesadillas</u>

INGREDIENTS:

1 box mac and cheese
4 large flour tortillas
1/4 cup shredded cheddar cheese
2 tablespoons butter

INSTRUCTIONS

Cook the mac and cheese according to the instructions on the box. Lay out the tortillas and divide the mac and cheese evenly among them, spreading it over half of each tortilla. Sprinkle shredded cheddar cheese over the mac and cheese. Fold the tortilla in half to create a quesadilla. Melt butter in a large skillet over medium-high heat. Place the quesadillas in the skillet and cook for 2-3 minutes on each side or until golden brown and the cheese is melted.

14. Mac and Cheese Stuffed Jalapenos

INGREDIENTS:

1 box mac and cheese
6-8 large jalapenos
1/4 cup bread crumbs
1/4 cup grated Parmesan cheese

INSTRUCTIONS

Preheat the oven to 375 degrees Fahrenheit. Cook the mac and cheese according to the instructions on the box. Cut off the stem end of the jalapenos and slice them in half lengthwise. Scoop out the seeds and membranes. Fill each jalapeno half with a spoonful of mac and cheese. In a small bowl, mix together the breadcrumbs and Parmesan cheese. Sprinkle the breadcrumb mixture over the top of each jalapeno half. Place on a baking sheet and bake for 20-25 minutes or until the jalapenos are tender and the cheese is melted.

15. Mac and Cheese Fritters

INGREDIENTS:

1 box mac and cheese
1/4 cup all-purpose flour
1/4 cup grated Parmesan cheese
1/4 teaspoon smoked paprika
Salt and pepper
2 tablespoons butter

INSTRUCTIONS

Cook the mac and cheese according to the instructions on the box. Let it cool for 5-10 minutes. Using a cookie scoop, form the mixture into fritters. In a separate bowl, combine the flour, Parmesan cheese, smoked paprika, salt, and pepper. Roll each fritter in the flour mixture until fully coated. Melt the butter in a large skillet over medium-high heat. Cook the fritters for 2-3 minutes on each side or until golden brown and crispy. Serve hot.

16. Mac and Cheese Pizza

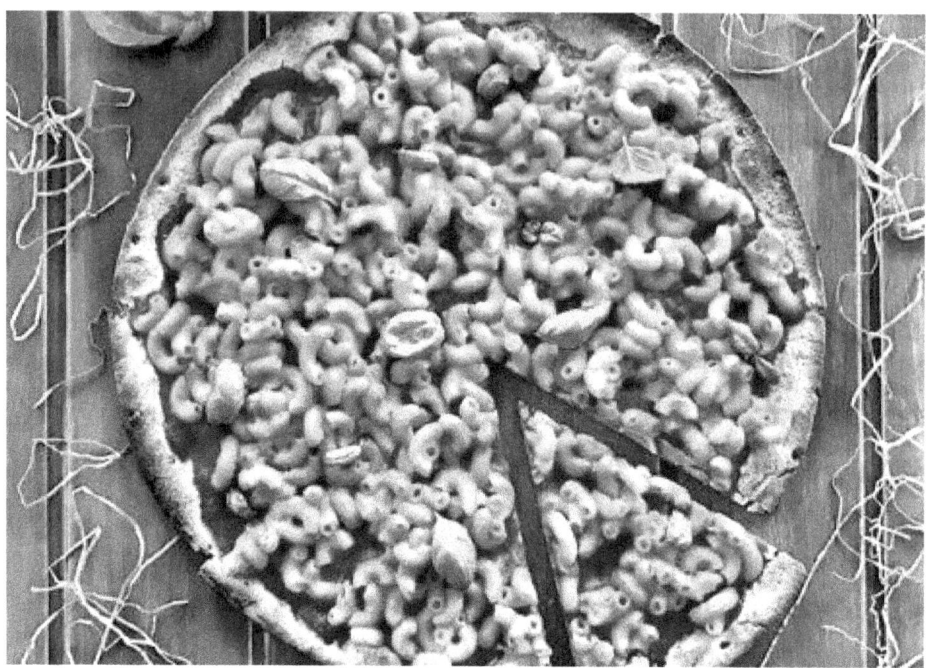

INGREDIENTS:

1 box mac and cheese
1 prepared pizza crust
1/2 cup pizza sauce
1 cup shredded mozzarella cheese

INSTRUCTIONS

Preheat the oven to 425 degrees Fahrenheit. Cook the mac and cheese according to the instructions on the box. Spread the pizza sauce over the pizza crust, leaving a 1/2-inch border around the edges. Spoon the mac and cheese over the pizza sauce. Sprinkle shredded mozzarella cheese over the top. Bake for 10-12 minutes or until the cheese is melted and bubbly.

17. Mac and Cheese Grilled Cheese

INGREDIENTS:

1 box mac and cheese
4 slices bread
4 slices cheddar cheese
2 tablespoons butter

INSTRUCTIONS

Cook the mac and cheese according to the instructions on the box. Toast the bread in a toaster or in a skillet. Place a slice of cheddar cheese on each slice of bread. Spoon the mac and cheese over one slice of bread. Top with the other slice of bread, cheese side down. Melt butter in a large skillet over medium-high heat. Place the sandwich in the skillet and cook for 2-3 minutes on each side or until golden brown and the cheese is melted.

18. **Mac and Cheese Dip**

INGREDIENTS:

1 box mac and cheese
1/2 cup sour cream
1/4 cup chopped green onions
1/4 teaspoon garlic powder
Salt and pepper

INSTRUCTIONS

Cook the mac and cheese according to the instructions on the box. Let it cool for 5-10 minutes. In a large bowl, mix together the mac and cheese, sour cream, green onions, garlic powder, salt, and pepper. Transfer the mixture to a small baking dish. Bake at 350 degrees Fahrenheit for 10-15 minutes or until hot and bubbly. Serve with tortilla chips or crackers.

19. Mac and Cheese Stuffed Mini Peppers

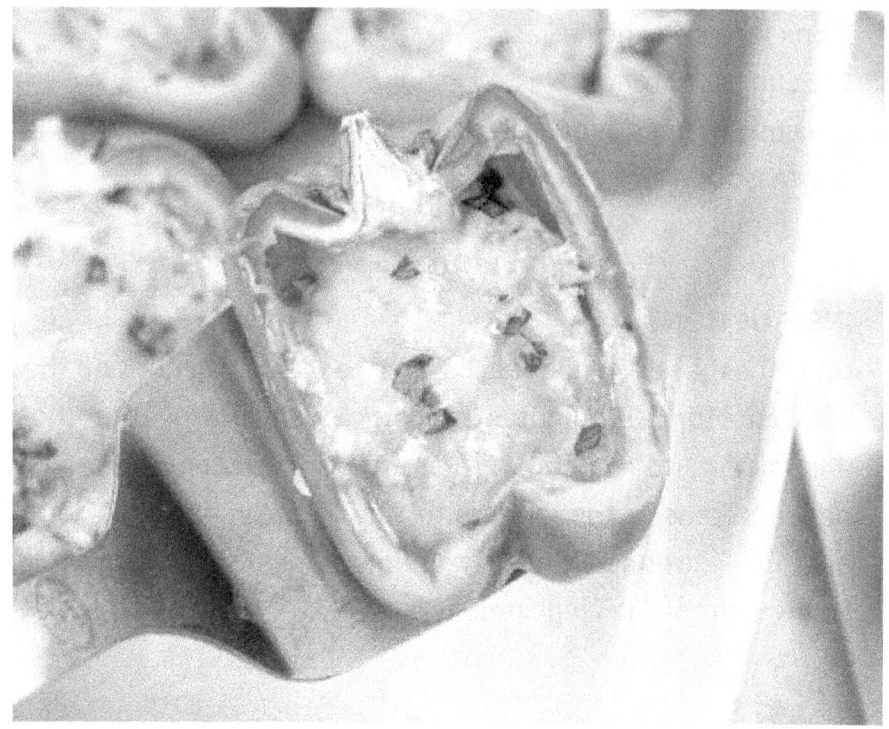

INGREDIENTS:

1 box mac and cheese
12-15 mini sweet peppers
1/4 cup shredded cheddar cheese
Salt and pepper

INSTRUCTIONS

Preheat the oven to 375 degrees Fahrenheit. Cook the mac and cheese according to the instructions on the box. Cut off the stem end of the mini peppers and remove the seeds and membranes. Fill each mini pepper with a spoonful of mac and cheese. Sprinkle shredded cheddar cheese over the top. Place on a baking sheet and bake for 15-20 minutes or until the peppers are tender and the cheese is melted.

20. Mac and Cheese Stuffed Tomatoes

INGREDIENTS:

1 box mac and cheese
6 large tomatoes
1/4 cup bread crumbs
1/4 cup grated Parmesan cheese

INSTRUCTIONS

Preheat the oven to 375 degrees Fahrenheit. Cut off the top of each tomato and scoop out the seeds and membranes. Cook the mac and cheese according to the instructions on the box. Fill each tomato with a spoonful of mac and cheese. In a small bowl, mix together the breadcrumbs and Parmesan cheese. Sprinkle the breadcrumb mixture over the top of each tomato. Place on a baking sheet and bake for 20-25 minutes or until the tomatoes are tender and the cheese is melted.

21. <u>Mac and Cheese Stuffed Zucchini</u>

INGREDIENTS:

1 box mac and cheese
2 large zucchini
1/4 cup shredded cheddar cheese
Salt and pepper

INSTRUCTIONS

Preheat the oven to 375 degrees Fahrenheit. Cut the zucchini in half lengthwise and scoop out the seeds and membranes.
Cook the mac and cheese according to the instructions on the box. Fill each zucchini half with a spoonful of mac and cheese. Sprinkle shredded cheddar cheese over the top. Place on a baking sheet and bake for 15-20 minutes or until the zucchini is tender and the cheese is melted.

22. <u>Mac and Cheese Croquettes</u>

INGREDIENTS:
1 box mac and cheese
1/4 cup flour
2 eggs
1/2 cup bread crumbs
1/4 cup grated Parmesan cheese
Salt and pepper

INSTRUCTIONS
Cook the mac and cheese according to the instructions on the box. Let it cool for 5-10 minutes. In a large bowl, mix together the flour, salt, and pepper. Using a spoon or cookie scoop, form the mac and cheese into small logs or cylinders. Dip each log into the flour mixture, then into the whisked eggs, then roll in the bread crumb mixture to coat. Place on a baking sheet and freeze for 15-20 minutes. Heat vegetable oil in a large skillet over medium-high heat. Fry the mac and cheese croquettes in batches for 2-3 minutes or until golden brown and crispy. Drain on paper towels.

23. Mac and Cheese Empanadas

INGREDIENTS:

1 box mac and cheese
1 package premade empanada dough
1/2 cup shredded cheddar cheese
1/4 cup chopped green onions

INSTRUCTIONS

Cook the mac and cheese according to the instructions on the box. Preheat the oven to 375 degrees Fahrenheit. Lay an empanada dough round on a flat surface. Spoon a small amount of mac and cheese onto one half of the dough. Sprinkle shredded cheddar cheese and chopped green onions over the top. Fold the other half of the dough over the filling and seal the edges with a fork. Repeat with remaining dough rounds and filling. Place on a baking sheet and bake for 15-20 minutes or until golden brown and crispy.

SALADS

24. <u>Garden Tuna Macaroni Salad</u>

Serving: 4 servings

INGREDIENTS

- 2 cups uncooked elbow macaroni
- 1 can (6 ounces) light water-packed tuna, drained and flaked
- 2/3 cup chopped sweet yellow pepper
- 2/3 cup chopped celery
- 1/2 cup shredded carrot
- 1/4 cup diced radishes
- 2 green onions, chopped
- 2 tablespoons minced fresh parsley
- 3/4 cup Miracle Whip
- 1/2 cup ranch salad dressing
- 1/4 cup grated Parmesan cheese
- 1 teaspoon coarsely ground pepper

Direction

a) Cook macaroni following package directions. As it cooks, mix parsley, vegetables, and tuna in a big bowl. Drain macaroni then rinse under cold water. Add into tuna mixture.

b) Mix pepper, parmesan cheese, ranch dressing, and miracle whip in a small bowl. Pour on salad, tossing until coated. Keep in fridge until serving time.

25. Seafood Macaroni Salad

YIELD: 10 SERVINGS

INGREDIENTS

1 teaspoon kosher salt, for boiling the pasta

3 cups dry elbow pasta (large or small will work)

1 cup mayonnaise OR cheese

¼ cup lemon juice

2 tablespoons yellow mustard

1 teaspoon Cajun seasoning

1 teaspoon Old Bay Seasoning

1 teaspoon minced garlic

1 pound cooked shrimp, peeled

1 pound imitation crab meat

¼ cup chopped green onion

⅓ cup diced celery

½ cup sliced black olives

1 tablespoon dried parsley flakes

DIRECTIONS

In a medium pot over high heat, bring water and salt to a boil. Add the pasta and cook until it's al dente. Drain the pasta once done, and rinse it under cold water to stop the cooking process.

In a large bowl, combine the mayonnaise, lemon juice, and mustard. Mix until well combined. Then sprinkle in the Cajun seasoning, Old Bay Seasoning, and garlic. Mix well.

Add the seafood and toss or stir in the bowl until it's covered with the dressing. Add the onions, celery, olives, and pasta. Fold all of the **INGREDIENTS**, sprinkle in the dried parsley flakes, and fold again. Cover the pasta and refrigerate for at least 1 hour before serving.

26. Mac and Cheese Salad with Bacon

INGREDIENTS:

1 box mac and cheese
1/2 cup cooked and crumbled bacon
1/4 cup chopped green onions
1/4 cup chopped cherry tomatoes
1/4 cup mayonnaise
1 tablespoon Dijon mustard
Salt and pepper to taste

INSTRUCTIONS

Cook the mac and cheese according to the instructions on the box. Allow to cool. In a separate bowl, mix together the mayonnaise, Dijon mustard, salt, and pepper. Add the cooked bacon, chopped green onions, and chopped cherry tomatoes to the cooled mac and cheese. Pour the mayonnaise mixture over the top and stir until everything is evenly coated.

27. **Southwest Mac and Cheese Salad**

INGREDIENTS:

1 box mac and cheese
1 can black beans, drained and rinsed
1/2 cup corn kernels
1/4 cup chopped red onion
1/4 cup chopped cilantro
1/4 cup salsa
1 tablespoon lime juice

INSTRUCTIONS

Cook the mac and cheese according to the instructions on the box. Allow to cool. In a separate bowl, mix together the black beans, corn kernels, chopped red onion, chopped cilantro, salsa, and lime juice. Add the cooled mac and cheese and stir until everything is evenly coated.

28. Mac and Cheese Salad with Ham and Peas

INGREDIENTS:

1 box mac and cheese
1/2 cup chopped cooked ham
1/2 cup frozen peas, thawed
1/4 cup chopped green onions
1/4 cup mayonnaise
1 tablespoon Dijon mustard

INSTRUCTIONS

Cook the mac and cheese according to the instructions on the box. Allow to cool. In a separate bowl, mix together the mayonnaise and Dijon mustard. Add the chopped ham, thawed peas, and chopped green onions to the cooled mac and cheese. Pour the mayonnaise mixture over the top and stir until everything is evenly coated.

29. <u>Caprese Mac and Cheese Salad</u>

INGREDIENTS:

1 box mac and cheese
1/2 cup chopped cherry tomatoes
1/2 cup chopped fresh mozzarella
1/4 cup chopped fresh basil
1/4 cup balsamic vinegar
Salt and pepper to taste

INSTRUCTIONS

Cook the mac and cheese according to the instructions on the box. Allow to cool. In a separate bowl, mix together the chopped cherry tomatoes, chopped fresh mozzarella, chopped fresh basil, balsamic vinegar, salt, and pepper. Add the cooled mac and cheese and stir until everything is evenly coated.

30. Bacon Ranch Mac and Cheese Salad

INGREDIENTS:

1 box mac and cheese
1/2 cup cooked and crumbled bacon
1/4 cup chopped green onions
1/4 cup chopped cherry tomatoes
1/4 cup ranch dressing

INSTRUCTIONS

Cook the mac and cheese according to the instructions on the box. Allow to cool. In a separate bowl, mix together the cooked and crumbled bacon, chopped green onions, chopped cherry tomatoes, and ranch dressing. Add the cooled mac and cheese and stir until everything is evenly coated.

31. Greek Mac and Cheese Salad

INGREDIENTS:

1 box mac and cheese
1/2 cup chopped cucumber
1/2 cup chopped cherry tomatoes
1/4 cup crumbled feta cheese
1/4 cup chopped kalamata olives
1/4 cup chopped red onion
2 tablespoons olive oil
1 tablespoon red wine vinegar
Salt and pepper to taste

INSTRUCTIONS

Cook the mac and cheese according to the instructions on the box. Allow to cool. In a separate bowl, mix together the chopped cucumber, chopped cherry tomatoes, crumbled feta cheese, chopped kalamata olives, chopped red onion, olive oil, red wine vinegar, salt, and pepper. Add the cooled mac and cheese and stir until everything is evenly coated.

32. **BLT Mac and Cheese Salad**

INGREDIENTS:

1 box mac and cheese
1/2 cup cooked and crumbled bacon
1/2 cup chopped cherry tomatoes
1/4 cup chopped romaine lettuce
1/4 cup mayonnaise
1 tablespoon Dijon mustard

INSTRUCTIONS

Cook the mac and cheese according to the instructions on the box. Allow to cool. In a separate bowl, mix together the mayonnaise and Dijon mustard. Add the cooked and crumbled bacon, chopped cherry tomatoes, and chopped romaine lettuce to the cooled mac and cheese. Pour the mayonnaise mixture over the top and stir until everything is evenly coated.

33. Italian Mac and Cheese Salad

INGREDIENTS:

1 box mac and cheese
1/2 cup chopped cherry tomatoes
1/2 cup chopped cooked Italian sausage
1/4 cup chopped fresh basil
1/4 cup chopped red onion
1/4 cup Italian dressing

INSTRUCTIONS

Cook the mac and cheese according to the instructions on the box. Allow to cool. In a separate bowl, mix together the chopped cherry tomatoes, chopped cooked Italian sausage, chopped fresh basil, chopped red onion, and Italian dressing. Add the cooled mac and cheese and stir until everything is evenly coated.

34. Mac and Cheese Salad with Broccoli and Bacon

INGREDIENTS:

1 box mac and cheese
1 cup chopped cooked broccoli
1/2 cup cooked and crumbled bacon
1/4 cup chopped green onions
1/4 cup mayonnaise
1 tablespoon Dijon mustard

INSTRUCTIONS

Cook the mac and cheese according to the instructions on the box. Allow to cool. In a separate bowl, mix together the mayonnaise and Dijon mustard. Add the chopped cooked broccoli, cooked and crumbled bacon, and chopped green onions to the cooled mac and cheese. Pour the mayonnaise mixture over the top and stir until everything is evenly coated.

35. Caesar Mac and Cheese Salad

INGREDIENTS:

1 box mac and cheese
1/2 cup chopped romaine lettuce
1/4 cup grated Parmesan cheese
1/4 cup Caesar dressing

INSTRUCTIONS

Cook the mac and cheese according to the instructions on the box. Allow to cool. In a separate bowl, mix together the chopped romaine lettuce, grated Parmesan cheese, and Caesar dressing. Add the cooled mac and cheese and stir until everything is evenly coated.

36. Mac and Cheese Salad with Tuna

INGREDIENTS:

1 box mac and cheese
1 can tuna, drained
1/4 cup chopped celery
1/4 cup chopped red onion
1/4 cup mayonnaise
1 tablespoon Dijon mustard

INSTRUCTIONS

Cook the mac and cheese according to the instructions on the box. Allow to cool. In a separate bowl, mix together the mayonnaise and Dijon mustard. Add the drained tuna, chopped celery, and chopped red onion to the cooled mac and cheese. Pour the mayonnaise mixture over the top and stir until everything is evenly coated.

SOUPS

37. Creamy Mac and Cheese Soup

INGREDIENTS:

1 box mac and cheese
2 cups milk
2 cups chicken broth
1/2 cup heavy cream
1/4 cup chopped green onions

INSTRUCTIONS

Cook the mac and cheese according to the instructions on the box. In a large pot, combine the cooked mac and cheese, milk, chicken broth, and heavy cream. Heat over medium heat, stirring occasionally, until heated through. Top with chopped green onions before serving.

38. Broccoli Cheddar Mac and Cheese Soup

INGREDIENTS:

1 box mac and cheese
1/2 cup chopped cooked broccoli
2 cups milk
2 cups chicken broth
2 cups shredded cheddar cheese

INSTRUCTIONS

Cook the mac and cheese according to the instructions on the box. In a large pot, combine the cooked mac and cheese, chopped cooked broccoli, milk, and chicken broth. Heat over medium heat, stirring occasionally, until heated through. Add shredded cheddar cheese and stir until melted and combined.

39. Tomato Mac and Cheese Soup

INGREDIENTS:

1 box mac and cheese
2 cups tomato juice
2 cups chicken broth
1/2 cup heavy cream
1/4 cup chopped fresh basil

INSTRUCTIONS

Cook the mac and cheese according to the instructions on the box. In a large pot, combine the cooked mac and cheese, tomato juice, chicken broth, and heavy cream. Heat over medium heat, stirring occasionally, until heated through. Top with chopped fresh basil before serving.

40. <u>Southwest Mac and Cheese Soup</u>

INGREDIENTS:

1 box mac and cheese
2 cups chicken broth
2 cups corn kernels
1 can black beans, drained and rinsed
1/2 cup chopped green onions
1/4 cup chopped fresh cilantro

INSTRUCTIONS

Cook the mac and cheese according to the instructions on the box. In a large pot, combine the cooked mac and cheese, chicken broth, corn kernels, drained and rinsed black beans, chopped green onions, and chopped fresh cilantro. Heat over medium heat, stirring occasionally, until heated through.

41. <u>Bacon Mac and Cheese Soup</u>

INGREDIENTS:

1 box mac and cheese
2 cups chicken broth
1 cup chopped cooked bacon
1/2 cup heavy cream
1/4 cup chopped green onions

INSTRUCTIONS

Cook the mac and cheese according to the instructions on the box. In a large pot, combine the cooked mac and cheese, chicken broth, chopped cooked bacon, heavy cream, and chopped green onions. Heat over medium heat, stirring occasionally, until heated through.

MAIN COURSE

42. Spicy Saucy Mac and "Cheese"

SERVES 4

INGREDIENTS:

12 ounces whole-grain elbow macaroni, cooked according to package directions, drained, and kept warm

1 batch No-Cheese Sauce

1½ teaspoons smoked paprika, or to taste

¼ teaspoon cayenne pepper, optional

INSTRUCTIONS

1. Preheat the oven to 350°F.
2. Place the cooked pasta in a large bowl. Add the No-Cheese Sauce, paprika, and cayenne pepper, if using, and mix well.
3. Spoon the mixture into a 9 × 13-inch baking dish and bake for 30 minutes, or until bubbly.

43. <u>Southwestern Mac and "Cheese"</u>

SERVES 4

INGREDIENTS:

1 medium yellow onion, peeled and diced
1 medium red bell pepper, seeded and diced
2 cups corn kernels (from about 3 ears)
1 jalapeño pepper, seeded and minced
2 teaspoons ground cumin
2 teaspoons ancho chile powder
Salt to taste
1 batch No-Cheese Sauce
2 cups cooked black beans, or one 15-ounce can, drained and rinsed
½ pound whole-grain elbow macaroni, cooked according to package directions, drained, and kept warm

INSTRUCTIONS

1. Preheat the oven to 350°F.
2. Place the onion and red pepper in a large saucepan and sauté over medium heat for 10 minutes. Add water 1 to 2 tablespoons at a time to keep the vegetables from sticking to the pan. Add the corn, jalapeño pepper, cumin, and chile powder and cook for 30 seconds. Remove from the heat and season with salt. Stir in the No-Cheese Sauce, beans, and cooked macaroni.
3. Spoon the mixture into a 9 × 13-inch baking dish and bake for 30 minutes, or until bubbly.

44. Homey Mac and Cheese

Makes: 8 servings

INGREDIENTS
- 2-1/2 cups uncooked elbow macaroni
- 1/4 cup butter, cubed
- 1/4 cup all-purpose flour
- 1/2 teaspoon salt
- 1/4 teaspoon pepper
- 3 cups 2% milk
- 5 cups shredded sharp cheddar cheese, divided
- 2 tablespoons Worcestershire sauce
- 1/2 teaspoon paprika

Directions

a) Preheat oven to 350°. Cook macaroni according to package Directions for al dente.

b) Meanwhile, in a large saucepan, heat butter over medium heat. Stir in flour, salt and pepper until smooth; gradually whisk in milk. Bring to a boil, stirring constantly; cook and stir until thickened, 2-3 minutes.

c) Reduce heat. Stir in 3 cups cheese and Worcestershire sauce until cheese is melted.

d) Drain macaroni; stir into sauce. Transfer to a greased 10-in. ovenproof skillet. Bake, uncovered, 20 minutes. Top with remaining cheese; sprinkle with paprika. Bake until bubbly and cheese is melted, 5-10 minutes.

45. Creamy Mac And Cheese With Crispy Bacon

INGREDIENTS

- 4 slices gluten-free bacon, chopped
- 1/2 small onion, grated
- 3 3/4 cups (880 ml) water
- 12 ounces (340 g) uncooked gluten-free elbow macaroni
- 1 1/2 teaspoons kosher or fine sea salt
- 1 can (12 ounces, or 340 g) evaporated milk
- 1 teaspoon dry mustard powder
- 1 teaspoon black pepper
- 1/2 teaspoon nutmeg (optional)
- 24 ounces (672 g) shredded extra-sharp cheddar cheese
- 8 ounces (227 g) shredded fontina or Monterey Jack cheese
- 2 ounces (56 g) grated Parmesan cheese
- Hot pepper sauce, to taste (optional)

METHOD

a) Press Sauté on your electric pressure cooker. When hot, add the bacon to the inner pot and cook, stirring, until crisp. Transfer to a paper towel–lined plate to cool. Remove all but 2 tablespoons (30 ml) of the fat from the inner pot. Add the onion and cook, stirring, until fully softened, about 5 minutes. Press Cancel.

b) Add the water, pasta, and salt to the inner pot. Stir and make sure the pasta is completely covered with the liquid. Close and lock the lid, making certain the steam release handle is in the sealing position. Cook on high pressure for 1 minute.

c) When it is finished, release the pressure naturally for 4 minutes, then slowly vent the remaining pressure by moving the handle between venting and sealing, letting out a little steam at a time. Use a hot pad to protect your hand. When all the steam is released, unlock the lid and open it carefully.

d) Test the pasta; it should be just tender and not too chewy. It will continue cooking as you finish making the dish. If it needs more time, set the lid back on the pressure cooker and let it rest for a few minutes.

e) Stir the milk, mustard powder, pepper, and nutmeg into the cooked pasta. Mix until evenly distributed. Add the cheeses, a little at a time, stirring until melted and creamy before adding more. Add a little hot pepper sauce if desired. If the sauce gets too thick, add 1/4 cup (60 ml) hot water or more to thin. Taste and adjust the seasonings if needed. Crumble the bacon and sprinkle on top; serve immediately.

46. Spinach and artichoke mac-and-cheese

SERVES: 6 TO 8

INGREDIENTS
- 6 tablespoons salted butter, at room temperature, plus more for greasing
- 1 (1-pound) box short-cut pasta, such as macaroni
- 2 cups whole milk
- 1 (8-ounce) package cream cheese, cubed
- 3 cups shredded sharp cheddar cheese
- Kosher salt and freshly ground pepper
- Ground cayenne pepper
- 2 cups packed fresh baby spinach, chopped
- 1 (8-ounce) jar marinated artichokes, drained and roughly chopped
- 1½ cups crushed Ritz crackers (about 1 sleeve)
- ¾ teaspoon garlic powder

Directions

a) Preheat the oven to 375°F. Grease a 9 × 13-inch baking dish.

b) In a large saucepan, bring 4 cups of salted water to a boil over high heat. Add the pasta and cook, stirring occasionally, for 8 minutes. Stir in the milk and cream cheese and cook until the cream cheese has melted and the pasta is al dente, about 5 minutes more.

c) Remove the pan from the heat and stir in 2 cups of the cheddar and 3 tablespoons of the butter. Season with salt, pepper, and cayenne. Stir in the spinach and artichokes. If the sauce feels too thick, add ¼ cup of milk or water to thin it.

d) Transfer the mixture to the prepared baking dish. Top with the remaining 1 cup of cheddar.

e) In a medium bowl, stir together the crackers, the remaining 3 tablespoons of butter, and the garlic powder. Sprinkle the crumbs evenly over the mac and cheese.

f) Bake until the sauce is bubbling and the crumbs are golden, about 20 minutes. Let cool for 5 minutes and serve. Store any leftovers refrigerated in an airtight container for up to 3 days.

47. Lobster Mac and Cheese

Servings Size: 2

INGREDIENTS
- 1 Tablespoons olive oil
- 3 lobster tails, split in half lengthwise and deveined
- 3 Tablespoons butter
- 2 Tablespoons flour
- 1 ½ cups half and half
- ½ cup milk
- ¼ teaspoons paprika
- ¼ teaspoons chili powder
- Salt to taste
- ¼ teaspoons Worcestershire sauce
- ½ cup grated Cheddar cheese
- 3 Tablespoons, grated Gruyere cheese
- 1 cup prepared elbow macaroni
- ½ cup Panko breadcrumbs
- ¼ cup melted butter
- 5 Tablespoons grated Parmesan cheese

Directions

a) Preheat the oven to 400 degrees.
b) Coat two gratin dishes with non-stick spray
c) Heat the oil in a skillet and brown the lobster tails for 2 minutes on medium heat.
d) Let the lobsters cool and separate the meat from the shells.
e) Chop the meat and discard the shells.
f) Use the same skillet to melt the butter.
g) Create a roux by stirring in the flour and continue stirring for 1 minute.
h) Pour in the half and half and milk and continue stirring for 3 minutes.
i) Let the liquid simmer and add the paprika, chili powder, salt, and Worcestershire Sauce.
j) Let simmer for 4 minutes.
k) Add the cheddar and Gruyere cheeses and stir for 5 minutes, until the cheese is melted.
l) Add the macaroni to the cheese sauce and gently stir in the lobster chunks.
m) Fill both gratin dishes with the mac and cheese mixture.
n) Combine the Panko, melted butter, and parmesan cheese in a bowl.
o) Drizzle the mixture over the mac and cheese.
p) Bake the mac and cheese for 15 minutes.

48. Camping Mac and Cheese

Makes: 3 servings

INGREDIENTS:
- 3 servings Rotelle pasta
- 2 Tablespoons butter or margarine
- 4 crushed cloves of garlic
- 4 Tablespoons spicy brown mustard
- 1 cup provolone cheese, grated salt and pepper milk
- Italian bread crumbs

INSTRUCTIONS

a) Melt butter and mix in garlic and mustard.
b) Cook pasta, and drain when al dente.
c) Return to pan and add mustard mix, cheese, salt and pepper.
d) At this point, dish can be heated briefly to melt cheese.
e) Or if you have an oven, place pasta in casserole dish, and pour in enough milk just until it begins to appear at edge of dish.
f) Top with Italian bread crumbs and bake for about half an hour at 350 degrees until bread crumbs brown up.

49. Mac and Cheese Cups

INGREDIENTS:
- 8 oz elbow macaroni
- 2 tbsp salted butter
- 1/4 teaspoons paprika (use smoked paprika if you have it)
- 2 tbsp flour
- 1/2 cup whole milk
- 8 oz sharp cheddar cheese grated
- chopped chives or scallions for garnish
- butter for greasing the pan

Directions:

g) Grease a non-stick: mini muffin pan very well with butter or non-stick: cooking spray. Preheat the oven to 400 degrees F.

h) Bring a pot of salted water to a boil over high heat, then cook the pasta for 2 minutes less than the package says.

i) Melt the butter and add the paprika. Add the flour and stir the mixture around for 2 minutes. While whisking, add the milk.

j) Remove the pot from the heat and add the cheeses and drained pasta, stirring it all together until the cheese and sauce are well distributed.

k) Portion your mac and cheese into the muffin cups, either with a spoon or a 3-tbsp cookie scoop.

l) Bake the mac and cheese cups for 15 minutes, until bubbling and gooey.

50. Queso Mac and Cheese

Makes: 8 Servings

INGREDIENTS:
- 1 pound of elbow macaroni
- Dash of salt and black pepper
- 12 ounces of American cheese, white
- 8 ounces of cheddar cheese, extra sharp
- 6 Tablespoons. of unsalted butter
- 6 Tablespoons. of all-purpose flour
- 4 cups of milk, whole
- 2, 8 ounce cans of tomatoes and green chiles, diced
- 1, 8 ounce can of green chiles, mild
- ½ cup of cilantro leaves, fresh and roughly chopped
- 1 cup of tortilla chips, crushed
- ½ teaspoons. of chili powder

INSTRUCTIONS
a) First, heat up the oven to 425 degrees.
b) While the oven is heating up, cook the pasta in a pot of water according to the directions on the package. Once the pasta is cooked, drain and set aside.
c) In a medium bowl, add in the American cheese and cheddar cheese. Stir well to mix.
d) Place a large Dutch oven over medium heat. Add in the unsalted butter. Once the butter is melted, add in the flour. Whisk until smooth and cook for 1 minute. Add in the milk and whisk to mix. Continue to cook for 8 minutes or until it has a thick consistency.
e) Add in the canned tomatoes and chiles. Cook for 2 minutes before removing from heat.
f) Add in 4 cups of the cheese mixture and stir well until smooth in consistency.
g) Add in the cooked pasta and cilantro. Toss well to mix and season with a dash of salt and black pepper.
h) Transfer this mixture to a large greased baking dish.
i) Add the tortilla chips, powdered chili, and remaining cup of cheese into a small bowl. Toss well to mix and sprinkle over the top of the pasta.
j) Place into the oven to bake for 12 to 15 minutes.
k) Remove and serve with a garnish of cilantro.

51. <u>Macaroni and Gruyere Cheese</u>

Makes: 8 Servings

INGREDIENTS:
- 1 pound of elbow macaroni
- 3 cups of gruyere cheese, grated
- 3 cups of half and half
- 4 egg yolks, large
- 3 Tablespoons. of unsalted butter
- Dash of salt

INSTRUCTIONS

a) First, heat up the oven to 325 degrees.

b) While the oven is heating up, place a large soup pot of salted water over medium to high heat. Bring the water to a boil. Once the water is boiling, add in the macaroni. Cook according to the directions on the package. Once cooked, drain the macaroni and rinse under running water. Drain and place into a large bowl.

c) Add in 2 and 2/3 cups of Gruyere cheese into the bowl with the cooked macaroni. Toss to mix.

d) Use a small bowl and add in the half and half, large egg yolks, and 3 tablespoons of melted butter. Stir well to mix and pour this mixture over the cooked pasta.

e) Transfer this mixture to a large baking dish. Cover with a sheet of aluminum foil.

f) Place into the oven to bake for 30 minutes. After this time remove the macaroni dish from the oven. Sprinkle the remaining Gruyere over the top.

g) Place back into the oven to bake for 20 to 25 minutes or until the top is golden.

h) Remove and serve immediately.

52. Macaroni and Cheese with Chicken

Makes: 4 Servings
Total Prep Time: 1 Hour and 20 Minutes

INGREDIENTS:
- 3 Tablespoons. of unsalted butter
- 1 ½ teaspoons of sea salt
- Dash of black pepper and salt
- ½ pound of penne pasta
- 1 Tablespoons. of olive oil, extra virgin
- 1 onion, small and thinly sliced
- 1 ½ cup of mozzarella cheese, smoked and grated
- 1 ½ cup of roast chicken, cooked and shredded
- 1 cup of Parmigiano-Reggiano Cheese, grated
- 1 Tablespoons. of rosemary, fresh and roughly chopped
- 3 Tablespoons. of all-purpose flour
- 2 ½ cups of milk, whole
- 2 cloves of garlic

INSTRUCTIONS
a) First, heat up the oven to 450 degrees. While the oven is heating up, butter a large baking dish.

b) Place a large pot filled with salted water over medium to high heat. Once the water is boiling, add in the penne pasta. Cook for 11 minutes or until the pasta is soft. Once soft. Drain the pasta and run under cold water. Drain the pasta again and place into a large bowl.

c) Place a medium skillet over medium heat. Add in the olive oil and once the oil is hot enough, add in the sliced onion and a pinch of sea salt. Cook for 10 minutes or until the onion is soft and golden. Add the onion to the pasta and toss to mix.

d) Add the mozzarella cheese, roast chicken, 2/3 cup of the parmesan cheese and fresh rosemary into the bowl with the pasta and onions. Toss to mix.

e) Use a medium saucepan and set over low to medium heat. Add in the butter. Once the butter is melted add in the all-purpose flour. Whisk for 3 minutes or until smooth. Then, add in the milk and continue to whisk until mixed.

f) Add in the cloves of garlic and 1 ½ teaspoons. of sea salt. Stir to mix and bring the mixture to a simmer. Reduce the heat to low and continue to cook while whisking until the mixture is thick in consistency. Toss out the cloves of garlic and add the sauce to the pasta.

g) Season with a dash of pepper. Toss to coat the pasta.

h) Transfer the mixture into the greased baking dish.

i) Sprinkle the remaining Parmesan cheese over the top and season with a dash of pepper.

j) Place into the oven to bake for 12 to 15 minutes or until gold. Remove and allow to sit for 15 minutes before serving.

53. Chili Mac Casserole

Ingredient

- 1 cup uncooked elbow macaroni
- 2 pounds lean ground beef (90% lean)
- 1 medium onion, chopped
- 2 garlic cloves, minced
- 1 can (28 ounces) diced tomatoes, undrained
- 1 can (16 ounces) kidney beans, rinsed and drained
- 1 can (6 ounces) tomato paste
- 1 can (4 ounces) chopped green chiles
- 1-1/4 teaspoons salt
- 1 teaspoon chili powder
- 1/2 teaspoon ground cumin
- 1/2 teaspoon pepper
- 2 cups shredded reduced-fat Mexican cheese blend
- Thinly sliced green onions, optional

Directions

a) Cook macaroni according to package directions. Meanwhile, in a large nonstick skillet, cook the beef, onion and garlic over medium heat until meat is no longer pink, breaking meat into crumbles; drain. Stir in the tomatoes, beans, tomato paste, chiles and seasonings. Drain macaroni; add to beef mixture.

b) Transfer to a 13x9-in. baking dish coated with cooking spray.

c) Cover and bake at 375° until bubbly, 25-30 minutes. Uncover; sprinkle with cheese. Bake until cheese is melted, 5-8 minutes longer. If desired, top with sliced green onions.

54. Spinach and artichoke mac-and-cheese bake

SERVES: 6 TO 8

INGREDIENTS
- 6 tablespoons salted butter, at room temperature, plus more for greasing
- 1 (1-pound) box short-cut pasta, such as macaroni
- 2 cups whole milk
- 1 (8-ounce) package cream cheese, cubed
- 3 cups shredded sharp cheddar cheese
- Kosher salt and freshly ground pepper
- Ground cayenne pepper
- 2 cups packed fresh baby spinach, chopped
- 1 (8-ounce) jar marinated artichokes, drained and roughly chopped
- 1½ cups crushed Ritz crackers (about 1 sleeve)
- ¾ teaspoon garlic powder

Directions

a) Preheat the oven to 375°F. Grease a 9 × 13-inch baking dish.

b) In a large saucepan, bring 4 cups of salted water to a boil over high heat. Add the pasta and cook, stirring occasionally, for 8 minutes. Stir in the milk and cream cheese and cook until the cream cheese has melted and the pasta is al dente, about 5 minutes more.

c) Remove the pan from the heat and stir in 2 cups of the cheddar and 3 tablespoons of the butter. Season with salt, pepper, and cayenne. Stir in the spinach and artichokes. If the sauce feels too thick, add ¼ cup of milk or water to thin it.

d) Transfer the mixture to the prepared baking dish. Top with the remaining 1 cup of cheddar.

e) In a medium bowl, stir together the crackers, the remaining 3 tablespoons of butter, and the garlic powder. Sprinkle the crumbs evenly over the mac and cheese.

f) Bake until the sauce is bubbling and the crumbs are golden, about 20 minutes. Let cool for 5 minutes and serve. Store any leftovers refrigerated in an airtight container for up to 3 days.

55. Monterrey Mini Mac and Cheese

Serving: 4

INGREDIENTS
- 8 ounces Whole-Wheat Macaroni
- ¾ cup Monterey Jack Cheese, shredded
- 2 cups Water

Directions

1. Place the macaroni and water in your pressure cooker. Seal the lid and cook on RICE mode for 8 minutes at High. Do a quick pressure release, and drain the macaroni. Return to the pressure cooker.

2. Stir in cheese, and cook on SAUTÉ at High, for 30 seconds until melted. Spoon between bowls, to serve.

56. Cauliflower Broccoli Macaroni

Servings: 6

INGREDIENTS:
- 2 cups cauliflower florets
- 1 oz American cheese, cut into pieces
- 3/4 cup coconut milk
- 1 cup cheddar cheese, shredded
- 8 oz elbow macaroni
- 2 cups broccoli florets
- 3 cups water
- 1/2 tsp salt

Directions:
1. Add water, macaroni, cauliflower, broccoli, and salt into the instant pot and stir well.
2. Seal pot with lid and cook on high for 4 minutes.
3. Release pressure using quick release method than open the lid.
4. Set instant pot on sauté mode. Add American cheese, coconut milk, and cheddar cheese. Stir well and cook for 5 minutes.
5. Serve and enjoy.

57. Spicy Chili Mac

Serving: 6 servings

INGREDIENTS

2 cups uncooked whole wheat elbow macaroni
1 pound lean ground turkey
1 small onion, chopped
2 to 3 jalapeno peppers, seeded and chopped
2 teaspoons olive oil
2 garlic cloves, minced
1 can (15 ounces) black beans, rinsed and drained
1 can (14-1/2 ounces) diced tomatoes, undrained
1 can (8 ounces) tomato sauce
1 to 2 tablespoons hot pepper sauce
2 to 3 teaspoons chili powder
1 teaspoon ground cumin
1/4 teaspoon cayenne pepper
1/4 teaspoon pepper
3/4 cup shredded reduced-fat cheddar cheese

Direction

Cook macaroni based on the package directions. In the meantime, use cooking spray to coat a large nonstick skillet, then put oil and cook in the jalapenos, onion and turkey on medium heat until meat is not pink. Mix in garlic; cook for a minute longer. Strain.

Stir in the seasonings, pepper sauce, tomato sauce, tomatoes and beans. Strain macaroni; add into turkey mixture. Then cook for 5 minutes over medium-low heat or until heated through.

Dust with cheese. Separate from heat; then cover and allow to stand until cheese is dissolved.

58. <u>Microwave Mac 'n' Cheese</u>

Serving: 4 servings

INGREDIENTS

2 cups uncooked elbow macaroni
2 cups hot water
1/3 cup butter, cubed
1/4 cup chopped onion
3/4 teaspoon salt
1/4 teaspoon pepper
1/4 teaspoon ground mustard
1/3 cup all-purpose flour
1-1/4 cups milk
8 ounces process cheese (Velveeta), cubed

Direction

Mix the first seven ingredients, in 2-qt. microwave-safe dish. Cover and set microwave to high power for 3 minutes. Remove and stir. Return cover and set microwave to 50% power; cook until boiling, about 3 minutes. In a bowl, mix milk and flour until smooth. Slowly stir flour mixture into macaroni. Add the cheese. Put cover back on and set on high power until macaroni is done and sauce is bubbling, 6-8 minutes. Stir every 3 minutes.

59. **Pizza Mac Cheese**

Serving: 6 servings

INGREDIENTS
- 1 package (7-1/4 ounces) macaroni and cheese dinner mix
- 6 cups water
- 1 pound ground beef
- 1 medium onion, chopped
- 1 small green pepper, chopped
- 11/2 cups shredded part-skim mozzarella cheese, divided
- 11/2 cups shredded cheddar cheese, divided
- 1 jar (14 ounces) pizza sauce
- 1/2 cup sliced pepperoni

Direction

Put the cheese packet from dinner mix aside. Bring water to a boil in a saucepan. Add in macaroni; cook for 8-10 minutes, until softened.

In the meantime, cook the green pepper, onion and beef in a large skillet on medium heat until no longer pink; drain.

Drain macaroni; and stir in the contents of cheese packet. Transfer to a round 2-1/2-qt. baking dish coated with grease. Sprinkle with 1/2 cup cheddar cheese and 1/2 cup mozzarella cheese. Put the pepperoni, pizza sauce, beef mixture, and leftover cheeses on top.

Bake without a cover for 30-35 minutes at 350 ° , until well heated.

60. Baked Three Cheese Macaroni

Serving: 12 servings

INGREDIENTS

1 package (16 ounces) elbow macaroni or fusilli pasta
6 tablespoons butter, cubed
1/2 cup all-purpose flour
4 cups 2% milk, warmed
4 cups shredded Gruyere cheese
2 cups shredded extra-sharp cheddar cheese
2 teaspoons salt
3/4 teaspoon freshly ground pepper
1/4 teaspoon freshly ground nutmeg
1 1/2 cups panko (Japanese) bread crumbs
1/2 cup grated Parmesan cheese
2 tablespoons butter, melted

Direction

Set oven to 350° to preheat. In a 6-quart stockpot, cook macaroni until al dente as directed on package. Drain off water; pour back into the pot.

Melt 6 tablespoons butter in a large saucepan over medium heat. Mix in flour until smooth; stir in warmed milk. Bring the mixture to a boil; stirring often; stir and cook until thickened, or for 2 to 3 minutes.

Put off the heat; mix in nutmeg, pepper, salt, Cheddar cheese, and Gruyere cheese. Mix in macaroni; toss well to coat.

Pour the pasta mixture into an oiled 13x9-inch baking dish. Combine bread crumbs with melted butter and Parmesan cheese and toss; scatter over the casserole. Baking without covering until bubbles appear and surface has turned golden brown, or for 30 to 40 minutes.

61. Makeover Slow Cooked Mac 'n' Cheese

Serving: 9 servings

INGREDIENTS

2 cups uncooked elbow macaroni
1 can (12 ounces) reduced-fat evaporated milk
1 1/2 cups fat-free milk
1/3 cup egg substitute
1 tablespoon butter, melted
8 ounces reduced-fat process cheese (Velveeta), cubed
2 cups shredded sharp cheddar cheese, divided
Coarsely ground pepper, optional

Direction

Cook the macaroni following the package instructions, then drain and wash it in cold water. Mix together the butter, egg substitute, milk and evaporated milk in a big bowl. Mix in the macaroni, 1 1/2 cups sharp cheddar cheese and process cheese.

Move to a cooking spray coated 3-quart slow cooker. Put cover on and cook for 2 to 3 hours on low until the middle becomes set, mixing once. Sprinkle with leftover sharp cheddar cheese and coarsely ground pepper (optional).

62. Slow Cooker Bacon Mac Cheese

Serving: 18 servings

INGREDIENTS

2 large eggs, lightly beaten
4 cups whole milk
1 can (12 ounces) evaporated milk
1/4 cup butter, melted
1 tablespoon all-purpose flour
1 teaspoon salt
1 package (16 ounces) small pasta shells
1 cup shredded provolone cheese
1 cup shredded Manchego or Monterey Jack cheese
1 cup shredded white cheddar cheese
8 bacon strips, cooked and crumbled

Direction

Whisk the first 6 ingredients in a big bowl until blended. Mix in cheeses and pasta; pour into a 4-5-quart slow cooker.

Put a cover on and cook on low until the pasta is soft, about 3-3-1/2 hours. Turn off the slow cooker, take out the mixture. Let sit without a cover for 15 minutes before eating. Sprinkle with bacon.

63. Bistro Mac Cheese

Serving: 8 servings

INGREDIENTS

1 package (16 ounces) uncooked elbow macaroni
5 tablespoons butter, divided
3 tablespoons all-purpose flour
2-1/2 cups 2% milk
1 teaspoon salt
1/2 teaspoon onion powder
1/2 teaspoon pepper
1/4 teaspoon garlic powder
1 cup shredded part-skim mozzarella cheese
1 cup shredded cheddar cheese
1/2 cup crumbled Gorgonzola cheese
3 ounces cream cheese, softened
1/2 cup sour cream
1/2 cup seasoned bread crumbs

Direction

Following package directions to cook macaroni then drain. In the meantime, melt 3 tbsp. of butter in a Dutch oven on low heat. Stir in flour until smooth, then whisk in seasonings and milk slowly.
Bring to a boil while stirring continuously, then cook and stir until thickened, about 2 minutes.
Lower heat and stir in cheeses until melted. Stir in sour cream, then put in macaroni, tossing to coat well. Heat leftover butter in a small skillet on moderate heat. Put in bread crumbs, then cook and stir until turn golden brown, then sprinkle over top of macaroni.

64. Makeover Creamy Mac Cheese

Serving: 10 servings

INGREDIENTS

1 package (16 ounces) elbow macaroni
1/3 cup all-purpose flour
1/2 teaspoon garlic powder
1/2 teaspoon pepper
1/4 teaspoon salt
2 cups fat-free half-and-half
2 tablespoons butter
2 cups fat-free milk
3 cups shredded reduced-fat sharp cheddar cheese

OPTIONAL TOPPING:

2 tablespoons butter
1 medium onion, chopped
5 cups cubed bread
1/2 cup shredded reduced-fat cheddar cheese

Direction

Set oven to heat to 350 degrees. Follow directions on package for cooking macaroni. Drain water from macaroni. In the meantime, stir until smooth half-and-half, flour, and seasonings in a mixing bowl. With the stove set to medium heat, melt butter in large pot. Whisk in the half-and-half/flour mixture. Stir in milk. Keep stirring and heat to a rolling boil. Immediately move away from heat. Stir in the cheese until it melts. Add macaroni and mix well. Place in a 13x9-in. grease pan. If topping is desired, place butter in a frying pan on medium-high heat. Put the onion in and stir constantly until soft. Mix in the cubes of bread and stir for another 2 minutes. Spread evenly over macaroni and sprinkle cheese on top. Do not cover; bake until heated, 25-30 minutes.

65. <u>Gruyère and Cheddar Mac and Cheese</u>

Makes: 6

INGREDIENTS:
- 1 cup half and half
- 1pounds gruyere cheese, grated and divided
- ⅓ cup seasoned breadcrumbs
- ½ stick of unsalted butter
- ¼ cup flour
- Parmigiano Reggiano to taste
- 1pound elbow macaroni, cooked
- Olive oil
- 1pound white cheddar, grated and divided
- 3 cups milk
- pinch of nutmeg
- Salt and freshly ground pepper to taste

INSTRUCTIONS

a) Preheat oven to 375 degrees.

b) Melt the butter, add the flour and whisk until well incorporated, making a roux.

c) Add the milk, slowly, whisking constantly for about 5 minutes until the sauce boils and thickens.

d) Add the half and half and cook for a little while longer to almost get thick again.

e) Take off the heat and add the salt, the pepper, the pinch of nutmeg, and the majority of the white cheddar and Gruyere. Mix everything until well incorporated.

f) Pour the sauce into the macaroni and stir. Top with the remaining Gruyere and white cheddar. Grate some Parmigiano Reggiano on top, to taste.

g) Sprinkle the breadcrumbs and bake for about 20 minutes or until the top is golden brown and the sauce is bubbly.

66. RumChata Macaroni and cheese

Servings: 4

INGREDIENTS
- 1 cup heavy whipping cream
- 1 cup rumchata
- 1/4 block grated mozzarella cheese
- ¼ block grated shark cheese
- ¼ block grated mile cheese
- 1 ½ sticks of butter
- 3 tablespoons sugar
- ½ teaspoon Slap Ya' Mama
- 3 tablespoons mustard
- ½ teaspoon garlic
- 1 pound bag of large elbow macaroni

INSTRUCTIONS

a) Bring the water to a boil and season with 1 tablespoon salt. Add the macaroni.

b) Boil macaroni in water until it is al dente, then drain and set aside.

c) Add all the remaining ingredients to a large pot.

d) Cook on the stovetop, on medium heat for a few minutes.

e) Stir constantly until smooth.

f) Pour this cheese mixture over the macaroni and mix well.

g) Put in the cooking dish, spread grated cheese on top, cover, and place in the oven for 25 minutes at 375 degrees.

h) Remove the cover and return to the oven for 10 more minutes.

i) Cool before serving.

j) Enjoy!

67. Soul Food Macaroni and Cheese

YIELD: 12 SERVINGS

INGREDIENTS

1 teaspoon kosher salt, for boiling the pasta
1 pound uncooked elbow pasta
4 tablespoons unsalted butter
2 tablespoons all-purpose flour
1½ cups half-and-half
1 cup evaporated milk
4 ounces cream cheese
8 ounces Gouda cheese, shredded or cubed
8 ounces Havarti cheese, shredded or cubed
1 teaspoon seasoning salt or plain kosher salt
1 teaspoon smoked paprika
1 teaspoon onion powder
1 teaspoon garlic powder
½ teaspoon freshly cracked black pepper
8 ounces sharp cheddar cheese, shredded
4 ounces mozzarella cheese, shredded
4 ounces Colby Jack cheese, shredded

DIRECTIONS

Preheat the oven to 350 degrees F.

In a large stockpot over high heat, pour about 2 quarts of water and sprinkle in the kosher salt. Bring the water to a boil, then add in the pasta. Cook the pasta until it is al dente (cooked but still firm), then drain the pasta and rinse it under cool water. Return the pasta to the stockpot and set to the side.

Place a large saucepan over medium heat, then toss in the butter. Melt the butter down completely, then sprinkle in the flour. Whisk the **INGREDIENTS** until they are well incorporated, then pour in the half-and-half and evaporated milk. Whisk the

INGREDIENTS and continue to cook over medium heat for about 3 minutes.

Reduce the heat to low, then add in the cream cheese, Gouda, and Havarti. Stir the mixture until the cheese melts and you have a nice, creamy cheese sauce. Sprinkle in the seasoning salt, paprika, onion powder, garlic powder, and pepper. Mix until well incorporated.

Pour the cheese sauce over the macaroni pasta in the stockpot. Stir everything until it is well combined, then pour half of the macaroni-and-cheese mixture into a 9-by-13-inch baking dish. Sprinkle half of the sharp cheddar, mozzarella, and Colby Jack on top of the mac and cheese. Next, add the remaining macaroni and cheese into the baking dish and top it off with the remaining cheese.

Bake the macaroni and cheese for 25 to 30 minutes. Remove from the oven and let sit for 5 to 10 minutes before serving.

68. Cheezy Tomato Macaroni

Makes 4 to 6 servings

- 1 tablespoon olive oil
- 1/2 cup finely chopped onion
- 2 garlic cloves, minced
- (14.5-ounce) can crushed tomatoes
- 1/2 teaspoon dried oregano
- 1/2 teaspoon dried basil
- Salt and freshly ground black pepper
- 8 ounces elbow macaroni
- 2 1/2 cups Mornay-Style Cheeze Sauce
- 1 ripe tomato, cut into 1/4-inch slices
- 2 tablespoons vegan Parmesan or Parmasio

In large skillet, heat the oil over medium heat. Add the onion and garlic, cover, and cook until soft, about 10 minutes. Stir in the tomatoes, oregano, and salt and pepper to taste. Reduce heat to low and simmer, uncovered, for 10 minutes. Set aside. Preheat the oven to 350°F. Lightly oil a 9 x 13-inch baking dish and set aside.

In a pot of boiling salted water, cook the macaroni over medium-high heat, stirring occasionally, until al dente, about 8 minutes. Drain well and return to the pot. Add the tomato mixture and the Mornay sauce and mix well. Transfer the mixture to the prepared baking dish. Top with the sliced tomato, fanning the slices around the perimeter of the casserole. Sprinkle with Parmesan.

Cover with foil and bake for 30 minutes. Uncover and continue baking until top is lightly browned, about 10 minutes longer. Serve immediately.

69. <u>Bacon Mac 'n' cheese</u>

SERVES 4

INGREDIENTS

350g short macaroni
8 rashers smoked streaky bacon (optional)
60g butter
60g plain flour
800ml milk
a dash of Worcestershire sauce
1 teaspoon English mustard
350g extra-mature Cheddar cheese, grated freshly ground black pepper

DIRECTIONS

Bring a large pan of lightly salted water to the boil and tip in the macaroni, stirring well to ensure it doesn't clump up. Boil until just tender but with plenty of bite, then drain and set aside.

Meanwhile, grill the bacon until crisp, if using. Chop it into snippets and set aside.

Melt the butter in a large saucepan set over a medium heat, then pour in the flour and stir thoroughly over the heat for a minute until you form a smooth roux. Reduce the heat to low and gradually add the milk, whisking constantly until you have dispersed the roux through the milk.

Turn the heat back up to medium and bring to a steady simmer, stirring all the time, until thickened, about 3–4 minutes.

Taste a little on the end of a teaspoon – it shouldn't taste floury at all; if it does, cook for another minute or so. Turn off the heat and stir through the Worcestershire sauce and mustard, and a generous grind of black pepper.

Sprinkle in about three-quarters of the cheese, stirring until it has melted, then add the cooked macaroni and bacon snippets and stir to combine.

Preheat the oven to 200°C/180°C Fan/Gas Mark 6. Spoon the macaroni into a baking dish and sprinkle over the remaining cheese. Bake in the hot oven for 15–20 minutes, until the top is golden and bubbling. Serve immediately.

70. <u>Phony Macaroni and Cheese</u>

Yields 4 servings

- 1 lb. tofu, firm - well-drained
- 2 cups cheddar cheese 2 eggs
- 1/4 cup heavy cream
- salt and pepper - to taste onion and garlic - to taste
- nutmeg - to taste
- dry mustard - to taste
- cayenne - to taste

DIRECTIONS

1. Drain tofu well, making sure to squeeze out all extra moisture, and slice into small pieces
2. (use a French fry cutter or equivalent for consistent sizes). In a separate bowl, mix together eggs, cream and cheese. Stir tofu pieces into mixture and add seasonings as desired. Transfer mixture to a casserole dish or greased pie plate and bake at 375 for 30 - 45 minutes or until golden brown.

71. Cauliflower & Tofu Mac and Cheese

Yields 4 servings

INGREDIENTS

- 16 ounces cauliflower, chopped into macaroni sized pieces
- 1 lb. tofu, firm - well-drained
- 2 cups cheddar cheese
- 2 eggs
- 1/4 cup heavy cream salt and pepper - to taste
- onion and garlic - to taste
- nutmeg - to taste
- dry mustard - to taste
- cayenne - to taste

DIRECTIONS

1   Drain tofu well, making sure to squeeze out all extra moisture, and slice into small pieces (use a French fry cutter or equivalent for consistent sizes).

2   In a separate bowl, mix together eggs, cream and cheese. Stir tofu pieces into mixture and add seasonings as desired.

3   Transfer mixture to a casserole dish or greased pie plate and bake at 375 for 30 - 45 minutes or until golden brown.

72. **One-Pot Turkey Chili Mac**

INGREDIENTS:
- 1 tablespoon coconut oil
- 1 pound ground turkey
- ½ teaspoon kosher salt
- ¼ cup onion, diced
- 2 stalks of celery, diced
- ½ cup bell pepper, diced
- 4 cups Chicken Bone Broth (2 cartons)
- 1 (16-oz) jar medium thick and chunky salsa
- 1 (15-16 oz) can reduced-sodium red kidney beans, drained
- 1 (1.25-oz) packet chili seasoning mix
- 8 ounces elbow macaroni
- 2 ounces cheddar cheese, diced
- 1 (8-oz) can no-salt-added tomato sauce
- Parsley leaves for garnishing

INSTRUCTIONS

a) Heat oil in a large saucepan over medium-high. Place ground turkey in the pan and season with salt. Cook 3-4 minutes, using your spatula to crumble the meat.

b) Stir in onion, celery, and bell pepper, cook for 2 more minutes until the turkey is cooked through. Add broth, salsa, beans, and seasoning mix. Bring to a boil.

c) Stir in pasta; cook for 8 minutes, stirring occasionally. Meanwhile, cut cheese into small cubes. Stir in tomato sauce and cook for 1 more minute. Serve the chili with cheese and parsley.

73. **Baked Mac And Cheeze**

Makes 4 to 6 servings

INGREDIENTS:

- 12 ounces elbow macaroni
- 3 tablespoons olive oil
- 1/2 cup minced onion
- 1/4 cup all-purpose flour
- ¾ cup nutritional yeast
- 2 1/2 cups plain unsweetened soy milk
- 1 tablespoon soy sauce
- 2 teaspoons white miso paste
- 1 teaspoon yellow mustard
- 1 teaspoon sweet paprika
- 1/2 teaspoon turmeric
- 1/2 teaspoon salt
- 1/8 teaspoon ground cayenne
- 3 tablespoons cornstarch
- 1 cup vegetable broth, homemade or store-bought

DIRECTIONS

In a pot of boiling salted water, cook the macaroni over medium-high heat until al dente, about 8 minutes. Drain and set aside. Preheat the oven to 375°F. Lightly oil a 3-quart casserole and set aside.

In a medium saucepan, heat 2 tablespoons of the oil over medium heat. Add the onion, cover, and cook 5 minutes, or until soft. Stir in the flour and the nutritional yeast and cook, uncovered, stirring, for 1 minute. Reduce heat to low, and slowly whisk in the soy milk. Continue to cook, stirring, until the mixture thickens. Stir in the soy sauce, miso, mustard, 1/2 teaspoon of the paprika, turmeric, salt, and cayenne.

In a small bowl, combine the cornstarch with the vegetable broth, stirring to blend. Stir the cornstarch mixture into the sauce and cook, stirring, until the sauce thickens. Taste, adjusting seasonings if necessary.

Combine the sauce and the cooked macaroni in the prepared casserole dish. Top with the bread crumbs and the remaining 1/2 teaspoon of paprika and drizzle with the remaining 1 tablespoon of oil. Bake until the mixture is hot and the crumbs are browned, about 30 minutes. Serve immediately.

74. Mac And Chard

Makes 4 to 6 servings

INGREDIENTS:

- 12 ounces elbow macaroni
- 1 medium bunch rainbow chard, tough stems removed and chopped
- 3 tablespoons olive oil
- 1/2 cup chopped yellow onion
- 1 garlic clove, chopped
- 1 medium Yukon Gold potato, peeled and cut into 1/4-inch slices
- Salt and freshly ground black pepper
- 2 cups vegetable broth, homemade
- ¾ teaspoon sweet paprika
- 1/2 cup unsalted roasted cashews
- 1 tablespoon fresh lemon juice
- 1 teaspoon Dijon mustard
- 1/2 cup dry bread crumbs

DIRECTIONS

In a pot of boiling salted water, cook the macaroni over medium-high heat until al dente, about 8 minutes. Drain well and set aside.

Steam the chard until tender, about 5 minutes. Set aside to cool. When cool enough to handle, squeeze any remaining moisture from the chard and set chard aside. Lightly oil a 9 x 13-inch baking dish and set aside. Preheat the oven to 350°F.

In a large saucepan, heat 2 tablespoons of the oil over medium heat. Add the onion, garlic, and potato. Season with salt and pepper to taste, cover, and cook until the vegetables are softened, about 10 minutes. Add 1 cup of the broth, the turmeric, and 1/2 teaspoon of the paprika and continue cooking, uncovered, until the vegetables are very soft. Remove from the heat and set aside.

Grind the cashews in a high-speed blender until ground to a fine powder. Add the onion and potato mixture, the remaining broth, lemon juice, mustard, and salt and pepper to taste and blend until smooth. Taste, adjusting seasonings if necessary.

Combine the sauce with the cooked macaroni and steamed chard and transfer to the prepared casserole. Sprinkle with the bread crumbs and remaining 1/4 teaspoon paprika and drizzle with the remaining 1 tablespoon of oil. Bake until hot and golden brown on top, about 30 minutes. Serve immediately.

75. Cheezy Tomato Macaroni

Makes 4 to 6 servings

- 1 tablespoon olive oil
- 1/2 cup finely chopped onion
- 2 garlic cloves, minced
- (14.5-ounce) can crushed tomatoes
- 1/2 teaspoon dried oregano
- 1/2 teaspoon dried basil
- Salt and freshly ground black pepper
- 8 ounces elbow macaroni
- 2 1/2 cups Mornay-Style Cheeze Sauce
- 1 ripe tomato, cut into 1/4-inch slices
- 2 tablespoons vegan Parmesan or Parmasio

In large skillet, heat the oil over medium heat. Add the onion and garlic, cover, and cook until soft, about 10 minutes. Stir in the tomatoes, oregano, and salt and pepper to taste. Reduce heat to low and simmer, uncovered, for 10 minutes. Set aside. Preheat the oven to 350°F. Lightly oil a 9 x 13-inch baking dish and set aside.

In a pot of boiling salted water, cook the macaroni over medium-high heat, stirring occasionally, until al dente, about 8 minutes. Drain well and return to the pot. Add the tomato mixture and the Mornay sauce and mix well. Transfer the mixture to the prepared baking dish. Top with the sliced tomato, fanning the slices around the perimeter of the casserole. Sprinkle with Parmesan.

Cover with foil and bake for 30 minutes. Uncover and continue baking until top is lightly browned, about 10 minutes longer. Serve immediately.

76. Chili Bean Mac

Serves: 4

INGREDIENTS:
- 1 lb. ground beef
- Salt and black pepper to taste
- ½ cup chopped onion
- 1 tsp minced garlic
- 1 (14 oz.) can dark red kidney beans, drained and rinsed
- 1 (15 oz.) can diced tomatoes and pepper
- 1 (8 oz.) can tomato sauce
- ½ cup dried macaroni
- ½ cup water
- 1 Tablespoons chili powder
- ½ tsp cumin powder
- 1 cup grated cheddar cheese
- Chopped fresh parsley for garnish

Directions

a) Add beef to a non-stick medium pot and cook for 10 minutes or until brown. Season with salt and black pepper.

b) Stir in onion and garlic; cook for 3 minutes or until onion is tender.

c) Pour in remaining **INGREDIENTS** except for parsley and cheddar cheese. Bring to a boil and then simmer for 15 to 20 minutes or until macaroni is al dente. Adjust taste with salt and black pepper.

d) Sprinkle cheddar cheese on top, cover pot and simmer for 1 to 2 minutes or until cheese melts.

e) Dish food and serve warm.

77. Italian Macaroni Bake

Makes: 6 servings

INGREDIENTS:
- 8 ounces uncooked elbow macaroni
- 1 pound ground beef, browned and drained
- salt and pepper, to taste
- 1 jar (14 ounces) pizza sauce
- 4-ounce can sliced mushrooms
- 2 cups grated mozzarella cheese

INSTRUCTIONS

a) Preheat oven to 350 degrees.

b) Cook macaroni according to package directions and drain.

c) Season cooked beef with salt and pepper. Place half the macaroni into bottom of a greased 2-quart baking dish.

d) Layer half each of the beef, pizza sauce, mushrooms, and cheese. Place remaining macaroni over top and repeat layers.

e) Cover and bake 20 minutes.

f) Uncover and bake 5–10 minutes more, or until cheese is melted.

78. <u>Macaroni and Mixed Cheese</u>

Makes: 12 Servings

INGREDIENTS:
- 1 teaspoon kosher salt, for boiling the pasta
- 1 pound uncooked elbow pasta
- 4 tablespoons unsalted butter
- 2 tablespoons all-purpose flour
- 1½ cups half-and-half
- 1 cup evaporated milk
- 4 ounces of cream cheese
- 8 ounces Gouda cheese, shredded or cubed
- 8 ounces Havarti cheese, shredded or cubed
- 1 teaspoon seasoning salt or plain kosher salt
- 1 teaspoon smoked paprika
- 1 teaspoon onion powder
- 1 teaspoon garlic powder
- ½ teaspoon freshly cracked black pepper
- 8 ounces sharp cheddar cheese, shredded
- 4 ounces mozzarella cheese, shredded
- 4 ounces Colby Jack cheese, shredded

INSTRUCTIONS

a) Preheat the oven to 350 degrees F.

b) In a large stockpot over high heat, pour about 2 quarts of water and sprinkle in the kosher salt. Bring the water to a boil, then add in the pasta. Cook the pasta until it is al dente (cooked but still firm), then drain the pasta and rinse it under cool water. Return the pasta to the stockpot and set it to the side.

c) Place a large saucepan over medium heat, then toss in the butter. Melt the butter down completely, then sprinkle in the flour. Whisk the **INGREDIENTS** until they are well incorporated, then pour in the half-and-half and evaporated milk. Whisk the

INGREDIENTS and continue to cook over medium heat for about 3 minutes.

d) Reduce the heat to low, then add in the cream cheese, Gouda, and Havarti. Stir the mixture until the cheese melts and you have a nice, creamy cheese sauce. Sprinkle in the seasoning salt, paprika, onion powder, garlic powder, and pepper. Mix until well incorporated.

e) Pour the cheese sauce over the macaroni pasta in the stockpot. Stir everything until it is well combined, then pour half of the macaroni-and-cheese mixture into a 9-by-13-inch baking dish. Sprinkle half of the sharp cheddar, mozzarella, and Colby Jack on top of the mac and cheese. Next, add the remaining macaroni and cheese to the baking dish and top it off with the remaining cheese.

f) Bake the macaroni and cheese for 25 to 30 minutes. Remove from the oven and let sit for 5 to 10 minutes before serving.

79. Gruyère and Cheddar Mac and Cheese

Makes: 6

INGREDIENTS:
- 1 cup half and half
- 1 pounds gruyere cheese, grated and divided
- ⅓ cup seasoned breadcrumbs (or panko breadcrumbs)
- ½ stick of unsalted butter
- ¼ cup flour
- Parmigiano Reggiano to taste
- 1 pounds elbow macaroni, cooked
- Olive oil
- 1 pounds white cheddar, grated and divided
- 3 cups milk
- pinch of nutmeg
- Salt and freshly ground pepper to taste

INSTRUCTIONS

a) Preheat oven to 375 degrees.

b) Melt the butter, add the flour and whisk until well incorporated, making a roux.

c) Add the milk, slowly, whisking constantly for about 5 minutes until the sauce boils and thickens.

d) Add the half and half and cook for a little while longer to almost get thick again.

e) Take off the heat and add the salt, the pepper, the pinch of nutmeg, and the majority of the white cheddar and Gruyere. Mix everything until well incorporated.

f) Pour the sauce into the macaroni and stir. Top with the remaining Gruyere and white cheddar. Grate some Parmigiano Reggiano on top, to taste.

g) Sprinkle the breadcrumbs and bake for about 20 minutes or until the top is golden brown and the sauce is bubbly.

80. Food Macaroni and Cheese

Makes: 12 Servings

INGREDIENTS

1 teaspoon kosher salt, for boiling the pasta
1 pound uncooked elbow pasta
4 tablespoons unsalted butter
2 tablespoons all-purpose flour
1½ cups half-and-half
1 cup evaporated milk
4 ounces cream cheese
8 ounces Gouda cheese, shredded or cubed
8 ounces Havarti cheese, shredded or cubed
1 teaspoon seasoning salt or plain kosher salt
1 teaspoon smoked paprika
1 teaspoon onion powder
1 teaspoon garlic powder
½ teaspoon freshly cracked black pepper
8 ounces sharp cheddar cheese, shredded
4 ounces mozzarella cheese, shredded
4 ounces Colby Jack cheese, shredded

INSTRUCTIONS

Preheat the oven to 350 degrees F.

In a large stockpot over high heat, pour about 2 quarts of water and sprinkle in the kosher salt. Bring the water to a boil, then add in the pasta. Cook the pasta until it is al dente (cooked but still firm), then drain the pasta and rinse it under cool water. Return the pasta to the stockpot and set to the side.

Place a large saucepan over medium heat, then toss in the butter. Melt the butter down completely, then sprinkle in the flour. Whisk the **INGREDIENTS** until they are well incorporated, then pour in the half-and-half and evaporated milk. Whisk the

INGREDIENTS and continue to cook over medium heat for about 3 minutes.

Reduce the heat to low, then add in the cream cheese, Gouda, and Havarti. Stir the mixture until the cheese melts and you have a nice, creamy cheese sauce. Sprinkle in the seasoning salt, paprika, onion powder, garlic powder, and pepper. Mix until well incorporated.

Pour the cheese sauce over the macaroni pasta in the stockpot. Stir everything until it is well combined, then pour half of the macaroni-and-cheese mixture into a 9-by-13-inch baking dish. Sprinkle half of the sharp cheddar, mozzarella, and Colby Jack on top of the mac and cheese. Next, add the remaining macaroni and cheese into the baking dish and top it off with the remaining cheese.

Bake the macaroni and cheese for 25 to 30 minutes. Remove from the oven and let sit for 5 to 10 minutes before serving.

81. Slap Ya' Mama Macaroni and cheese

Servings: 4

INGREDIENTS
- 1 cup heavy whipping cream
- 1 cup half and a half
- 1/4 block grated mozzarella cheese
- ¼ block grated shark cheese
- ¼ block grated mile cheese
- 1 ½ sticks of butter
- 3 tablespoons sugar
- ½ teaspoon Slap Ya' Mama
- 3 tablespoons mustard
- ½ teaspoon garlic
- 1 pound bag of large elbow macaroni

INSTRUCTIONS
- Bring the water to a boil and season with 1 tablespoon salt. Add the macaroni.
- Boil macaroni in water until it is al dente, then drain and set aside.
- Add all the remaining **INGREDIENTS** to a large pot.
- Cook on the stovetop, on medium heat for a few minutes.
- Stir constantly until smooth.
- Pour this cheese mixture over the macaroni and mix well.
- Put in the cooking dish, spread grated cheese on top, cover, and place in the oven for 25 minutes at 375 degrees.
- Remove the cover and return to the oven for 10 more minutes.
- Cool before serving.
- Enjoy!

82. Spinach and artichoke mac-and-cheese bake

SERVES: 6 TO 8

INGREDIENTS
- 6 tablespoons salted butter, at room temperature, plus more for greasing
- 1 (1-pound) box short-cut pasta, such as macaroni
- 2 cups whole milk
- 1 (8-ounce) package cream cheese, cubed
- 3 cups shredded sharp cheddar cheese
- Kosher salt and freshly ground pepper
- Ground cayenne pepper
- 2 cups packed fresh baby spinach, chopped
- 1 (8-ounce) jar marinated artichokes, drained and roughly chopped
- 1½ cups crushed Ritz crackers (about 1 sleeve)
- ¾ teaspoon garlic powder

Directions

g) Preheat the oven to 375°F. Grease a 9 × 13-inch baking dish.

h) In a large saucepan, bring 4 cups of salted water to a boil over high heat. Add the pasta and cook, stirring occasionally, for 8 minutes. Stir in the milk and cream cheese and cook until the cream cheese has melted and the pasta is al dente, about 5 minutes more.

i) Remove the pan from the heat and stir in 2 cups of the cheddar and 3 tablespoons of the butter. Season with salt, pepper, and cayenne. Stir in the spinach and artichokes. If the sauce feels too thick, add ¼ cup of milk or water to thin it.

j) Transfer the mixture to the prepared baking dish. Top with the remaining 1 cup of cheddar.

k) In a medium bowl, stir together the crackers, the remaining 3 tablespoons of butter, and the garlic powder. Sprinkle the crumbs evenly over the mac and cheese.

l) Bake until the sauce is bubbling and the crumbs are golden, about 20 minutes. Let cool for 5 minutes and serve. Store any leftovers refrigerated in an airtight container for up to 3 days.

83. Cauliflower Broccoli Macaroni

Servings: 6
Cooking Time: 9 minutes

INGREDIENTS:

- 2 cups cauliflower florets
- 1 oz American cheese, cut into pieces
- 3/4 cup coconut milk
- 1 cup cheddar cheese, shredded
- 8 oz elbow macaroni
- 2 cups broccoli florets
- 3 cups water
- 1/2 tsp salt

Directions:

1. Add water, macaroni, cauliflower, broccoli, and salt into the instant pot and stir well.
2. Seal pot with lid and cook on high for 4 minutes.
3. Release pressure using quick release method than open the lid.
4. Set instant pot on sauté mode. Add American cheese, coconut milk, and cheddar cheese. Stir well and cook for 5 minutes.
5. Serve and enjoy.

84. Monterrey Mini Mac and Cheese

Serving: 4

INGREDIENTS
- 8 ounces Whole-Wheat Macaroni
- ¾ cup Monterey Jack Cheese, shredded
- 2 cups Water

Directions
1. Place the macaroni and water in your pressure cooker. Seal the lid and cook on RICE mode for 8 minutes at High. Do a quick pressure release, and drain the macaroni. Return to the pressure cooker.
2. Stir in cheese, and cook on SAUTÉ at High, for 30 seconds until melted. Spoon between bowls, to serve.

85. Almond Macaroni and Cheese

MAKES 6 to 8

INGREDIENTS
- 2 cups almond milk
- 4 tablespoons flour
- 4 tablespoons butter
- 2 lbs. extra sharp cheddar cheese
- 1 lb. elbow macaroni

DIRECTIONS
a) Cook elbow macaroni. Drain well
b) Grate cheddar cheese
c) Melt butter over medium heat
d) Add flour to create a roux
e) Warm milk. Add grated cheese to milk to create a thick slurry
f) Add macaroni to cheese
g) Mix cheese and macaroni. Top macaroni and cheese.
h) Bake 350 °F until brown and bubbly

86. Queso Mac and Cheese

Makes: 8 Servings

INGREDIENTS:
- 1 pound of elbow macaroni
- Dash of salt and black pepper
- 12 ounces of American cheese, white
- 8 ounces of cheddar cheese, extra sharp
- 6 Tablespoons. of unsalted butter
- 6 Tablespoons. of all-purpose flour
- 4 cups of milk, whole
- 2, 8 ounce cans of tomatoes and green chiles, diced
- 1, 8 ounce can of green chiles, mild
- ½ cup of cilantro leaves, fresh and roughly chopped
- 1 cup of tortilla chips, crushed
- ½ teaspoons. of chili powder

INSTRUCTIONS

l) First, heat up the oven to 425 degrees.

m) While the oven is heating up, cook the pasta in a pot of water according to the directions on the package. Once the pasta is cooked, drain and set aside.

n) In a medium bowl, add in the American cheese and cheddar cheese. Stir well to mix.

o) Place a large Dutch oven over medium heat. Add in the unsalted butter. Once the butter is melted, add in the flour. Whisk until smooth and cook for 1 minute. Add in the milk and whisk to mix. Continue to cook for 8 minutes or until it has a thick consistency.

p) Add in the canned tomatoes and chiles. Cook for 2 minutes before removing from heat.

q) Add in 4 cups of the cheese mixture and stir well until smooth in consistency.

r) Add in the cooked pasta and cilantro. Toss well to mix and season with a dash of salt and black pepper.

s) Transfer this mixture to a large greased baking dish.

t) Add the tortilla chips, powdered chili, and remaining cup of cheese into a small bowl. Toss well to mix and sprinkle over the top of the pasta.

u) Place into the oven to bake for 12 to 15 minutes.

v) Remove and serve with a garnish of cilantro.

87. **Macaroni and Gruyere Cheese**

Makes: 8 Servings

INGREDIENTS:
- 1 pound of elbow macaroni
- 3 cups of gruyere cheese, grated
- 3 cups of half and half
- 4 egg yolks, large
- 3 Tablespoons. of unsalted butter
- Dash of salt

INSTRUCTIONS

i) First, heat up the oven to 325 degrees.

j) While the oven is heating up, place a large soup pot of salted water over medium to high heat. Bring the water to a boil. Once the water is boiling, add in the macaroni. Cook according to the directions on the package. Once cooked, drain the macaroni and rinse under running water. Drain and place into a large bowl.

k) Add in 2 and 2/3 cups of Gruyere cheese into the bowl with the cooked macaroni. Toss to mix.

l) Use a small bowl and add in the half and half, large egg yolks, and 3 tablespoons of melted butter. Stir well to mix and pour this mixture over the cooked pasta.

m) Transfer this mixture to a large baking dish. Cover with a sheet of aluminum foil.

n) Place into the oven to bake for 30 minutes. After this time remove the macaroni dish from the oven. Sprinkle the remaining Gruyere over the top.

o) Place back into the oven to bake for 20 to 25 minutes or until the top is golden.

p) Remove and serve immediately.

88. Macaroni and Cheese with Chicken

Makes: 4 Servings
Total Prep Time: 1 Hour and 20 Minutes

INGREDIENTS:
- 3 Tablespoons. of unsalted butter
- 1 ½ teaspoons of sea salt
- Dash of black pepper and salt
- ½ pound of penne pasta
- 1 Tablespoons. of olive oil, extra virgin
- 1 onion, small and thinly sliced
- 1 ½ cup of mozzarella cheese, smoked and grated
- 1 ½ cup of roast chicken, cooked and shredded
- 1 cup of Parmigiano-Reggiano Cheese, grated
- 1 Tablespoons. of rosemary, fresh and roughly chopped
- 3 Tablespoons. of all-purpose flour
- 2 ½ cups of milk, whole
- 2 cloves of garlic

INSTRUCTIONS

k) First, heat up the oven to 450 degrees. While the oven is heating up, butter a large baking dish.

l) Place a large pot filled with salted water over medium to high heat. Once the water is boiling, add in the penne pasta. Cook for 11 minutes or until the pasta is soft. Once soft. Drain the pasta and run under cold water. Drain the pasta again and place into a large bowl.

m) Place a medium skillet over medium heat. Add in the olive oil and once the oil is hot enough, add in the sliced onion and a pinch of sea salt. Cook for 10 minutes or until the onion is soft and golden. Add the onion to the pasta and toss to mix.

n) Add the mozzarella cheese, roast chicken, 2/3 cup of the parmesan cheese and fresh rosemary into the bowl with the pasta and onions. Toss to mix.

o) Use a medium saucepan and set over low to medium heat. Add in the butter. Once the butter is melted add in the all-purpose flour. Whisk for 3 minutes or until smooth. Then, add in the milk and continue to whisk until mixed.

p) Add in the cloves of garlic and 1 ½ teaspoons. of sea salt. Stir to mix and bring the mixture to a simmer. Reduce the heat to low and continue to cook while whisking until the mixture is thick in consistency. Toss out the cloves of garlic and add the sauce to the pasta.

q) Season with a dash of pepper. Toss to coat the pasta.

r) Transfer the mixture into the greased baking dish.

s) Sprinkle the remaining Parmesan cheese over the top and season with a dash of pepper.

t) Place into the oven to bake for 12 to 15 minutes or until gold. Remove and allow to sit for 15 minutes before serving.

89. Meatballs and shortcut macaroni

Ingredient

- 1 Onion finely cut
- 1 cup Diced celery
- 2 Carrots; cut any way you like, up to 3
- 2 tablespoons Tomato puree
- 3 cups Water
- Salt
- Pepper
- Bay leaf
- 2 tablespoons Oil; up to 3
- 1 pounds Minced meat; (the best is turkey)
- 1 slice Chala soaked; drained and mashed
- 3 Eggs
- Some flour

Directions:

a) Gravy: in a big pot heat the oil, add onion, celery, carrots, tomato puree, water and spices and simmer. Meantime prepare the meatballs.

b) Meatballs: Combine and form meatballs about 12-14. Roll in flour and drop in the boiling gravy. Cook for 40 minutes on low flame. Make sure you have enough liquids, you'll need them for the macaroni.

c) Boil 250-400 (½-⅔ pound) short cut macaroni for ⅔ of the recommended time. Bake for 20-30 till hot

90. <u>Macaroni and Cheese Meatloaf</u>

Makes: 6

INGREDIENTS:
- 4 ounces cooked macaroni
- 1 pound hamburger
- ½ cup soft bread crumbs
- ½ cup milk
- 2 eggs, slightly beaten
- ½ cup chopped onion
- 2 tablespoons chopped green pepper
- ⅓ cup grated Cheddar cheese
- 1 teaspoon salt
- ½ teaspoon pepper

INSTRUCTIONS

a) Cook macaroni according to instructions on package.
b) Preheat oven to 350 degrees F.
c) Mix together macaroni, hamburger, bread crumbs, milk, eggs, onion, green pepper, cheese, salt and pepper. Shape into loaf.
d) Bake for 1 hour.

91. Macaroni in Creamy Beef Sauce

Servings per Recipe: 6

INGREDIENTS
- 1 (16 oz.) package elbow macaroni
- 1/2 cup sour cream
- 1 lb. ground beef
- 1/2 cup pesto

Directions

a) In a large pan of lightly salted boiling water, add the macaroni and cook for about 8-10 minutes or till desired doneness and drain well and keep aside.

b) In a large skillet, heat oil on medium-high heat and cook beef for about 5-7 minutes or till browned and drain the all grease.

c) Add the cream and pesto and stir to combine.

d) Cook till warmed completely.

e) Stir in the macaroni and serve immediately.

92. Macaroni with strawberries

YIELDS 5 Servings

INGREDIENTS
- Macaroni of your choice
- 3 cups strawberries, fresh or frozen
- 1 cup plain plant-based yogurt, coconut cream, or Greek plant-based yogurt
- sugar to taste

Directions

a) Follow the package directions for making pasta of your choice.

b) Wash and remove the stems from the strawberries. Chop some strawberries to put on top of the dish.

c) In a blender, combine the remaining strawberries, cream or plant-based yogurt, sugar, and vanilla extract.

d) If you want a chunkier sauce, mash the strawberries with a fork or mix them in batches, giving the last strawberries a brief blitz with the blender.

e) Toss the cooked macaroni with the strawberry sauce. It's delicious hot or cold.

93. <u>Pastitsio</u>

Makes 6 servings

INGREDIENTS
- 3 cups cooked or 2 (15.5-ounce) cans chickpeas, drained and rinsed
- 12 ounces elbow macaroni
- 1 tablespoon olive oil
- 1 medium yellow onion, chopped
- 2 garlic cloves, chopped
- 1 (10-ounce) package frozen chopped spinach, thawed
- 1/2 teaspoon dried oregano
- 1/2 teaspoon ground cinnamon
- 1/2 teaspoon dried mint
- 1/4 cup dry white wine
- 2 cups marinara sauce, homemade (see Marinara Sauce) or store-bought
- 2 tablespoons chopped fresh flat-leaf parsley
- Salt and freshly ground black pepper
- 2 cups Vegan White Sauce
- 1/2 cup chopped pine nuts

Directions

In a food processor, pulse the chickpeas until coarsely chopped and set aside.

In a pot of boiling salted water, cook the macaroni over medium-high heat, stirring occasionally, until al dente, about 8 minutes. Drain well and set aside. Preheat the oven to 375°F. Lightly oil a 9 x 13-inch baking dish and set aside.

In a large skillet, heat the oil over medium heat. Add the onion and garlic, cover, and cook until softened, about 5 minutes. Stir in the spinach, chopped chickpeas, oregano, cinnamon, mint, and wine and simmer, uncovered, for 3 minutes. Stir in the tomato sauce, parsley, and salt and pepper to taste. Cook over low heat for 10 minutes to blend flavors.

Spread half of the cooked pasta in the prepared baking dish and spread the tomato-chickpea sauce on top. Spread the remaining pasta on top of the tomato-chickpea sauce and top the pasta with the white sauce. Sprinkle with pine nuts.

Cover with foil and bake for 30 minutes. Uncover and bake 10 minutes longer. Let stand at room temperature for 10 minutes before serving.

DESSERT

94. Macaroni souffle

Makes: 5 servings

INGREDIENTS:
18 ounces Macaroni
3 ounces Gouda Cheese
18 ounces Ground Beef
1 Onion
1 can Pureed Tomatoes, small
1 pack White Sauce

INSTRUCTIONS
Cook the noodles according to directions. 2.Fry the meat with the chopped onions and the tomato puree in a skillet until meat is crumbly. Season with Salt and Pepper to taste. 3.Grease a souffle pan and alternate noodles and meat mix in it. 4.Make the sauce according to directions and pour over all. 5.Cook in 200 C oven for 30 minutes.

95. Mac and Cheese Ice Cream

INGREDIENTS

1 box mac and cheese
1 cup heavy cream
1 cup whole milk
1/2 cup sugar
1 tsp vanilla extract

INSTRUCTIONS Cook the mac and cheese according to the instructions on the box. In a separate pot, combine the heavy cream, whole milk, sugar, and vanilla extract. Heat over medium heat, stirring occasionally, until the sugar dissolves. Add the cooked mac and cheese to the pot and stir until well combined. Remove from heat and let cool. Pour the mixture into an ice cream maker and churn according to the manufacturer's instructions.

96. Mac and Cheese Bread Pudding

INGREDIENTS

1 box mac and cheese
4 cups cubed day-old bread
4 eggs
2 cups whole milk
1/2 cup sugar
1 tsp vanilla extract

INSTRUCTIONS Cook the mac and cheese according to the instructions on the box. In a separate bowl, whisk together the eggs, whole milk, sugar, and vanilla extract. Add the cubed bread and cooked mac and cheese to the bowl and stir until well combined. Pour the mixture into a greased 9x13-inch baking dish. Bake at 350°F for 45-50 minutes, or until the top is golden brown and the center is set.

97. Mac and Cheese Cheesecake

INGREDIENTS

1 box mac and cheese
2 cups cream cheese, softened
1 cup sugar
4 eggs
1 tsp vanilla extract

INSTRUCTIONS Cook the mac and cheese according to the instructions on the box. In a separate bowl, beat together the cream cheese and sugar until smooth. Add the eggs one at a time, beating well after each addition. Stir in the cooked mac and cheese and vanilla extract. Pour the mixture into a greased 9-inch springform pan. Bake at 350°F for 45-50 minutes, or until the center is set.

98. Mac and Cheese Blondies

INGREDIENTS

1 box mac and cheese
1/2 cup unsalted butter, melted
1 cup brown sugar
2 eggs
1 tsp vanilla extract
1 cup all-purpose flour
1/2 tsp salt
1/2 cup white chocolate chips

INSTRUCTIONS

Cook the mac and cheese according to the instructions on the box. In a separate bowl, whisk together the melted butter and brown sugar. Add the eggs and vanilla extract and whisk until smooth. Stir in the cooked mac and cheese. Add the flour and salt and stir until just combined. Fold in the white chocolate chips. Pour the mixture into a greased 9x13-inch baking dish. Bake at 350°F for 25-30 minutes, or until a toothpick inserted into the center comes out clean. Let cool before slicing into squares.

99. Mac and Cheese with Berry Compote

INGREDIENTS:
- 1 cup heavy cream
- 1 1/2 cups whole milk
- 4 cloves, whole
- 1 pinch nutmeg
- 2 teaspoons cinnamon, plus more for sprinkling
- 3 tablespoons sugar, plus more for sprinkling
- 1/8 teaspoon vanilla extract
- 1 box pasta, shape of your choice
- 1/3 cup all-purpose flour
- 1/3 cup unsalted butter
- 1 pinch kosher salt
- 1 (8 ounces) container mascarpone
- Berry compote
- Whipped cream
- Vanilla ice cream

Preheat oven to 375°F.
Combine cream, milk, spices, sugar, and vanilla in a small saucepan, and heat on low to infuse flavors, about 10 minutes.
Bring a pot of salted water to a boil. Cook pasta for 2 minutes less than recommended cooking time. Strain, and run cold water through it to stop cooking.
In a medium saucepan, combine butter and flour and cook to create a roux. Once the roux comes together, keep cooking until butter starts to brown and is fragrant.
When the roux is done, add milk mixture in batches through a strainer while whisking. Continue adding, cooking, and whisking until your sauce won't thicken anymore.
Turn heat off and stir in mascarpone. Add pasta and stir to combine.
Transfer mixture to a 9x13 baking dish, sprinkle the top liberally with cinnamon and sugar, and bake* for 15-20 minutes, until bubbling.
Serve with fresh berry compote, whipped cream, and/or vanilla ice cream.

100. Mac and Cheese with Apple and Brioche

Ingredients:
- 3 tbsp sugar
- 1 vanilla pod
- 100 g macaroni
- 200 ml whole milk
- 3 egg yolks
- 1 tbsp sugar
- 100 g cheddar cheese, grated
- 1 Bramley apple
- 50 g brioche crumbs

INSTRUCTIONS

Heat a medium saucepan of water and add 3 tbsp of sugar. Slice the vanilla pod in half, scrape out the seeds and add half of them to the water with half of the pod. When the water is boiling add the pasta, stir and cook for about 8 minutes, until just cooked through.

Heat the milk with the remaining half of the vanilla seeds and pod. Whisk the egg yolks with the 1tbsp of sugar, then slowly pour over the hot milk, whisking continuously. Pour the mix back into the saucepan and stir over medium heat until it thickens. Remove from the heat and add the grated cheese. Stir it in until it's completely melted.

Tip the cooked pasta into the sauce and combine well.

Peel and core the apple. Slice it in half, then cut it into 2mm slices. Preheat a grill to high.

In ramekins or small ovenproof dishes, spoon a little of the mac n' cheese mixture to fill it almost halfway. Arrange a layer of the raw apple slices, then top with more mac n' cheese. Finish with a topping of brioche crumbs and a little extra grated cheese.

Place the ramekins under the grill for a minute or two, until the bread and cheese are crisp and golden. Serve.

CONCLUSION

In conclusion, mac and cheese is a timeless classic that will never go out of style. Its simple yet satisfying flavors have made it a staple in kitchens around the world for generations. Whether you prefer it homemade or from a box, there's no denying the appeal of a steaming bowl of mac and cheese. So the next time you're in need of a comforting meal, whip up a batch of mac and cheese and savor the warm and cheesy goodness.

www.ingramcontent.com/pod-product-compliance
Lightning Source LLC
Chambersburg PA
CBHW070353120526
44590CB00014B/1116